W9-DCC-656

# CHARLES ALBERT FECHTER

# CHARLES ALBERT FECHTER

BY

KATE FIELD

With Illustrations

BENJAMIN BLOM    New York/London

DEDICATED

## 𝕿𝖔 𝖙𝖍𝖊 𝕸𝖊𝖒𝖔𝖗𝖞

OF

# CHARLES DICKENS

First Published 1882
Reissued 1969 by
Benjamin Blom, Inc., Bronx, New York 10452
and 56 Doughty Street, London, W.C. 1

Library of Congress Catalog Card Number 70-82827

Printed in the United States of America

# CONTENTS.

———◦◦◦———

# LIST OF ILLUSTRATIONS.

# FECHTER IN EUROPE.

## 1824–1869.

# CHARLES ALBERT FECHTER

## IN EUROPE.

——◦◦⦂◦⦂◦◦——

### 1824–1869.

GENIUS is no more a matter of accident than the rising of the sun. Though genius dazzle with the unexpected brilliancy of a comet, like the comet it has its regular orbit, and when the science of art has been discovered, as it will be ere the dawn of the millennium, the world will know the cause as well as the effect of human greatness.

Blood tells under all circumstances, and never has it told a more straightforward story than in the character of Charles Albert Fechter, in whose ancestors we see the beginnings of himself. It is not a little significant that his mother bore the kingly name of Regis, with which name, too, royalty took personal interest, it being an old Piedmontese custom that the king should stand sponser to the twelfth child of any of his subjects. Now it happened that Fechter's maternal grandfather was the twenty-first of twenty-six children ; consequently the king became godfather to his twelfth and twenty-

fourth great-grand-uncles !   Italian by birth, this grandfather was equally Italian in his profession of carver,
yet not so Italian but he could make his home in
Flanders, where Fechter's mother, Marie Angélique
Regis, was born.   Arcaçhon, France, was the birth-
place of his father, Jean Maria Guillaume Fechter, his
paternal grandfather being a native of Cologne and of
German lineage.   This grandfather's tendencies were
likewise in the direction of art.   He found congenial
employment in polishing court-suit buttons and in
making sword-handles, the latter of which occupations
was not scorned by Benvenuto Cellini.

The alphabet of art having been acquired by Fechter's grandparents, it was not strange that they should
bequeath greater abilities to their children.   Jean Maria Fechter was not only an excellent sculptor, but a
born comedian, who, however, confined his acting to
private life ; while his wife, whom he married in Lisle,
was more than usually gifted.   Though uneducated,
she possessed literary and artistic tastes, writing verses
and stories of considerable feeling and deftly turning
her fingers to account by the manufacture of artificial
flowers.   She would take the delicate, almost impalpa-
ble tissue that lines the shells of eggs, and, fashioning
it into roses, would simultaneously color and scent
them with rose-water.   But these flowers were too
fragile for mortal use, so Madame Fechter resorted to
stouter material.   Born of Piedmontese parents, she
spoke no Italian, very little Flemish, and adopted the
language of her husband's chosen home, France.

Gallic as was Fechter *père* in all his feelings, he

never became naturalized. Receiving an offer from Storr and Mortimer, the great jewellers of England, to take the position of the well-known sculptor Tamissier, whose unfortunate habits had rendered him unfit for work, Jean Fechter moved from Paris to London, where, in Hanway Yard, Oxford Street, Charles Albert Fechter was born October 23, 1824. He was the youngest but one of thirteen children, eleven of whom died in infancy. With artistic proclivities on both sides of the house, — with the hot blood of Italy, the speculative blood of Germany, strongly impregnated with French *verve*, flowing through his veins,—it is not strange that Charles Fechter, "the man without a country," should belong to all the world, which Shakespeare tells us is a stage. Learning to read at a very early age, his passion for the drama evinced itself in peculiar theatrical monologues, and in devotion to Shakespeare, — the plays of "Hamlet," "Othello," and "Macbeth" being especial favorites. Appropriating garments belonging to his parents, the youthful Roscius was in the habit of retiring to an unoccupied room where, after locking the door, he blackened his nose and arrayed himself in motley attire. Thus, half-way 'twixt man and woman, he spouted and strutted, to the great terror of the mice and the infinite satisfaction of himself. During these private exhibitions Fechter dedicated his energies to tragedy, but, being endowed with great vivacity, relieved himself, when off duty, by jumping on chairs and tables, drawing caricatures, and playing monkey for the delectation of visitors. Not content with his own interpretation of imaginary heroes, Fechter's passion frequently overcame Fechter's conscience, and many of his father's valuable coins were secretly disposed of in order that, like a bad little cherub, he might sit up aloft among the gods of Drury Lane. There Fechter feasted his eyes and ears on Macready, Charles Kemble, the elder Vandenhoff and the elder Wallack, recollections of whom he retained to his death. Of the four, Charles Kemble, with his charmingly natural acting, was his favorite, and Vandenhoff his " cold blanket." Wallack made a great impression upon him, and Macready delighted him in " William Tell." But the artist of all others whom he worshipped was Malibran. She often held her young lover on her knee, little knowing the amount of sentiment she had inspired in an eight-year-old boy. Poor Malibran ! that she with her great heart and great genius should have married a great brute and died neglected !

Sent to Templeton's College at the age of eight, Fechter stood very well, showing great aptitude for Greek and Latin, great fondness for history, — although he never could retain a name or a date, — and despising every branch of mathematics. Largely endowed with imagination, young Fechter entertained his teachers with marvellous stories of adventure, and, magnetizing them as he later magnetized larger audiences in more romantic situations, enjoyed their favor to an unusual extent. Of course a lad of Fechter's mettle could not but be attractive to the bullies of his school, who, true to their prerogative, set upon him in numbers and nicknamed him " French frog." Stung to the quick by this taunt, Fechter resented it, but, fighting single-handed, was always worsted. " Only come on one at a time and I 'll whip every one of you," said Fechter ; but no, the bullies preferred to attack him in a body, and so the " French frog " vowed vengeance. Way-laying the leading persecutor one day, he thoroughly whipped his adversary ; the bullies cried " quits," and ever after treated the " French frog " like a true Briton.

England, with all its virtues, was not France to Fechter *père*, who in 1830 once more found himself in Paris ; but the Revolution came, and the unhappy sculptor was again driven across the Channel. Though but six years old, Fechter remembered seeing the great Mademoiselle Georges act, and being carried over the barricades on his father's shoulders. This abortive attempt at migration served to endear Paris still more to Jean Fechter's heart, and the failure of 1830 became a *fait accompli* in 1836. Poor as the father was, — the time had been when he had broken up chairs to serve for firewood, — he sent Charles to school at Boulogne-sur-Seine ; but at the end of two years the boy returned home to aid in supporting the family. Assisting his father in making bronzes and candelabras, studying French with Hersant his drawing-master, reading the classics, and dreaming of the theatre which he fre-quented with the constancy of a passionate lover, Charles led a busy life for two years, and at sixteen became the hero of a duel. How did it happen? Foolishly, of course. Taken to the Café Militaire by a friend much older than himself, — a captain in the army, — young Fechter listened to stories of prowess

until, excited by wine and cigars most unwisely given
to him, he too longed for an opportunity to prove his
courage. The subject of duelling being introduced,
there was no man present but could revive some wonderful affair of so-called honor in which he had either
killed or wounded his opponent. At least young
Fechter could fight a duel if some one would be good
enough to insult him ; and, flushed with the insidious
thief that steals away even the best of brains, he found
an enemy in his friend and host. Taking offence at a
trifling remark, the aspiring youth slapped the face of
Monsieur le Capitaine with his own epaulet and demanded the satisfaction of a gentleman. Badly as the
Captain felt, he was forced by that *noblesse,* which so
frequently obliges people to make fools of themselves,
to accept the challenge. As the challenged party he of
course had the choice of weapons, and selected the rapier. With pistols Fechter might kill the Captain ;
with rapiers the Captain could kill Fechter, but *would*
not. So the two met, with their seconds, in that Bois
de Boulogne of other days, when it was a gloomy forest
sacred to duellists and highwaymen. " Coward ! " was
Fechter's salutation to his friend ; " you have selected
the rapier because you know you are master of it.
With pistols the chances would have been more even.
At least I can call you Coward, and from my soul I do
so." Coward indeed ! The Captain's only fear was
lest, in giving the " satisfaction " for which Hotspur
panted, he should not be sufficiently expert to draw the
minimum of blood. These fears were realized when
Fechter's rapier fell and the blood flowed from his

wrist. The wound, though severe, was not dangerous, and Fechter, having fought his duel and learned how unjust he had been to the Captain, forgot his grievance, embraced his enemy, and was taken home alive to his terrified parents. Would that all equally absurd duels ended as happily !

From the Bois de Boulogne to the Salle Molière, from duelling to private theatricals, seems a long step, yet none too long for Fechter, who in this same year, 1840, made his first appearance behind those footlights by which he had been dazed. The Salle Molière is a small theatre in the Passage Molière, which at that time was used by St. Aulaire, —a famous ·teacher of acting, Rachel's first instructor, — and let once a week to amateurs for private theatricals. Theirs was a unique company, changing with each performance and singularly enough brought together. A list of the pieces to be played being put up, any one by selecting his part and paying for it — the amount charged being in proportion to the importance of the character — could strut his brief hour upon the stage. Such a republican form of government would lead to eminently doleful results in this country, where actors are made, not born ; but France is ·not America. There, it is said, all men and women are actors by nature, and the worst become professional.

This company of the Salle Molière was eminently successful, — so much so that Fechter's brother-in-law, himself an ardent admirer of the drama, paid the young sculptor's fee, and put his name down for the *jeune premier* in Dumas's "Le Mari de la Veuve." The amount expended for acting was returned in tickets, so that the aspiring amateurs were always sure of an audience. Fechter's success was so great that he soon became a necessity to the company, one of whose members, now a distinguished diplomatist, (diplomacy is but another name for acting), insisted upon paying Fechter's fees in order that he might be " stirred up " by contact with so magnetic and admirable an actor.

After seeing Fechter perform, St. Aulaire came up with a strange gentleman, saying, " My boy, if you will come to my *cours* (class), I will teach you for nothing." " And if you make the stage your profession, I will give you all my parts," added the unknown, who turned out to be no other than Scribe ! Fechter could not accept St. Aulaire's generous offer, for the reason that his father required his assistance in the studio ; but he did not forget the great compliment paid him by the first of professors and the first of playwrights, and longed for emancipation.

Temporary release soon came. At this time Duvernoir, a well-known singer, now a professor in the Conservatoire of Paris, was organizing a company for Florence, Italy, and at the last moment lost his juvenile actor, Gaston, who was unexpectedly drafted into the army. Remembering the great ability displayed by Fechter at the Salle Molière, Duvernoir offered him the vacant situation. A winter in Florence, all the " interesting lovers," and a salary combined ! The offer proved irresistible, and in spite of fatherly expostulation the stage-struck youth set off for Italy in January, 1841.

To dream of acting and to act are sadly different, as *le jeune premier* soon found to his cost. Starting with a modest wardrobe, he made the mournful discovery that his requirements greatly exceeded his possessions, and straightway developed latent abilities in tailoring and boot-making. Fechter not only made his own dresses, but cut those of actors as impecunious as himself. But top-boots, — what should he do for these very expensive and very necessary articles? The question was father to the answer. Is not genius ever equal to an emergency? What should he do for top-boots? Why, invent them, of course! So out of thin oil-cloth Fechter manufactured a pair of boots of so stylish a cut and perfect a fit as to be the envy of his associates. Love-making in those top-boots must have possessed a double fascination. It could not have been bootless. Ah, and there was that crowning glory of man, a hat! Silk hats are a poor man's natural enemy, yet a lover without a good-looking hat is about as impossible as a pretty woman without a head of hair. But had not Fechter an old hat? What could be easier than to wet it whenever necessary and make it shine like the rising sun? Those home-made clothes, those ingenious boots, and that deceitful hat carried Fechter through his season in Italy, perhaps for the very good reason that the season was not much longer than his original top-boots. Never had Florence known such a winter. The oldest inhabitant went mad in endeavoring to conjure up the ghost of a like recollection. Almanacs were in vain. July invaded January, and the snow on the Apennines, melted by the hot breath of summer, vanished into thin air. Of what avail to perform French comedy at the *Cocomero* (" Watermelon"), when the astonished Florentines were longing with tragic thirst to eat their accustomed watermelons in the streets? Moreover, there was a rival French troupe at another theatre. One might have survived; the two killed each other.

Nevertheless, Manager Duvernoir persevered in his enterprise for six weeks, and Fechter won praise from the Sir Hubert Stanleys of the period. Strange to say, every play advertised was by Scribe. Those were the good old days of Austrian surveillance, when grand dukes held their court, and censors supervised public morals. Dumas was their *bête noire*, Molière was sniffed at, but Scribe was considered harmless; so Scribe became the author of "Tartuffe," wore Dumas's colors, and displayed a versatility never known before or since. There was no press to tell tales, the censors nursed their blissful ignorance, and the knowing public enjoyed the joke.

Fechter enjoyed a joke of quite a different hue. Returning one night from the theatre, he was assaulted by a thief who, attracted by a very large stage jewel, — a diamond-paste pin which he supposed to be real, — thought it easy work to rob so slight a youth. Fechter's hot blood and practised muscle soon undeceived the robber, who, upon finding himself at a disadvantage, drew a dirk. What was to be done? Fechter spoke not one word of Italian; the robber not one word of French. The language of pantomime was common to both however, and they acted out the following dialogue.

" O strike, if you like," gesticulated Fechter; " I'm entirely unarmed, and you can have it all your own way; but as you want nothing of me but my diamond pin, it is hardly worth while killing me, when you can have it on easier terms."

" How so ? " asked the robber.

" Why, I'll make an exchange. Give me that cameo in your shirt-bosom, and I'll give you my diamond."

" You're a queer sort of fellow," replied the robber. " I rather like you. It's a bargain."

Whereupon the exchange took place. Actor and robber shook hands and separated, — the former in possession of a very beautiful cameo, the latter sole proprietor of pinchbeck ! What that robber did to himself, upon discovering how completely the tables had been turned, remains a mystery. Certainly Fechter never acted better than on this occasion.

At the end of the six weeks Manager Duvernoir, poor in pocket and in spirits, called his company together, declared himself bankrupt, paid a few cents on a dollar, and dismissed his friends with a tearful blessing. With characteristic generosity Fechter divided his share among the humbler actors, who expressed their gratitude by immediately decamping with a portion of his wardrobe. Penniless, Fechter applied for aid to a banker friend, proposing to leave his clothes, books, etc. as security. Believing the *jeune premier's* word to be as good as his bond, the banker lent him money and gave him a draft on a Marseilles house for one thousand francs. Thus fortified, Fechter started for France with the virtuous intention of making no use of the draft; but Fechter was young, and found as great difficulty in keeping as in making money. Marseilles was attractive, he might never travel again, and so in Marseilles he remained until his purse became an aching void, and the letter of credit his only friend. Presenting this letter he was received with unaccountable "effusion." "My dear fellow," exclaimed the banker, seizing Fechter's hands and wringing them vigorously, — "my dear fellow, I am delighted to see you. It's a boy, I tell you it's a boy, and such a boy! A marvel! You never saw anything like it in your life and you never will, take my word for it. Money? Certainly. Any amount you please to name. I never was so happy in all my life. There! there's the amount, and to think it's a boy!"

Entirely bewildered by this extraordinary conduct, Fechter wondered whether he were dealing with an escaped lunatic. He became convinced of it upon finding that the banker asked for no receipt. On suggesting its advisability to the banker the latter replied: "Bless my soul, certainly. Did n't I take a receipt? Well, it's a boy you know, and how can I think of anything else? There now, it's all right; here's what belongs to you, and I'm the happiest man in the world!" "Well, he is mad," thought Fechter, as he walked away; "a raving maniac," he added, when, upon opening the package, he discovered his receipt! Returning, Fechter apprised the banker of his mistake, and handed back the important voucher. "Great Heaven!" he exclaimed, "you don't say so? *Did* I do that? Well, well, — it's a boy and a beauty. We haven't yet decided upon a name, but I'll write you all about it for I'm sure you'll want to know." And again the happy banker took an affectionate farewell of his young customer with the final explanation that the " boy " was his first child !

It was a welcome day to Fechter's parents when the prodigal son returned. " No more theatre," said the father ; " I want you to be a sculptor." So Fechter became a student of the Académie des Beaux Arts, working there every evening after spending his days over bronzes in his father's studio. Work, however, did not lessen his love of fun, which found many an outlet. One night he, in company with equally exuberant students, locked up an *écrivain public* (letter-writer for the ignorant poor) in his portable box of a shop, and, wheeling him off, left him several miles from his beat. The little man pounded, the little man scolded, the little man did his best to get out of the window ; but little as he was, the window was less, and there in solitude and rage he passed the night, no police coming to his rescue until the next morning. Unable to give any explanation of his strange situation, the little man got the credit of temporary insanity, — a verdict of great popularity with all juries averse to investigation.

Fechter's thoughts never failed to return to his first love, for it was during this same year, 1841, that he entered the Conservatoire with the determination of studying for the Théâtre Français. He aspired to grand rôles, and wished to base his style on classic models. Fired with ambition, he went before his judges. First among the inquisitors came Professor Provost, who eyed young Hotspur with disdainful pity. Those who knew the broad-shouldered, full-chested Fechter can hardly think of him as a very thin, very long, and sentimentally delicate youth; yet such was his appearance in 1841.

"Now, sir," said the grim professor, "what do you want?"

"I want to be an actor."

"An actor, indeed! Permit me to assure you that acting is out of the question. You've no lungs, sir; you are consumptive, sir; and my advice to you is to take a great deal of exercise. When you walk, throw your coat open and your shoulders back, put your thumbs in the armholes of your vest, and take long respirations. If you follow my advice you may live, but you can never be an actor."

Conscious of power, and by no means persuaded that the gods loved him sufficiently to mark him for an early death, Fechter ran the gauntlet of the entire Conservatoire. Michelot was his next critic.

"Eh bien, what will you recite?"

"I am up in *Séide* of Voltaire's 'Mahomet.'"

"That will do very well. Allons."

Sitting up after the manner of orchestral conductors, Michelot made an imaginary baton of his right arm and began to beat time as if the performance were operatic, and the youth before him a tenor about to sing his first romanza. This was too much for Fechter, whose eyes and ears were of the quickest, whose sense of humor

was most acute, and whose audacity was almost un-
paralleled in the annals of the stage. Acting upon the
impulse of the moment he carried out Michelot's suggestion, rushed forward with operatic gesticulation, sang
Voltaire's hexameters, and turned heavy tragedy into
laughable burlesque. The effect upon Michelot can
be more readily imagined than described. There was
nothing to be said, because this suiting the voice to
Michelot's action was too clever and appropriate a
satire for words, especially as those present enjoyed the
joke immensely.

In his third trial Fechter stood up before Samson.

"You will attempt *Séide*," said Samson. "Very
well, begin at the fourth act."

"But, M. Samson," remonstrated the youth, "I'd
rather begin at the beginning. I must get warmed up
before I can do my best in that act."

"Nonsense," replied Samson. "You ought to be
able to begin anywhere. Let me have the fourth act."

Obeying the sovereign command, Fechter plunged
*in medias res*, going through the dramatic interview between *Séide* and *Palmire* as far as the question, "Qui?
Zopire?" in scene fourth. Giving this with all the
dramatic intensity demanded by the situation, the young
tragedian was taken aback by Samson's interruption:
"Plus bête, mon ami, plus bête. 'Qui? Zopire?'
doit être plus bête!"

"I really cannot say it like you, sir," replied Fechter,
and the rebellious youth was ordered down.

Last came Beauvallet, with whom Fechter had much
better success, being allowed to go through *Séide* with-

out comment. " That will do," said Beauvallet, " you are quite as bad as any of those at the Théâtre Français," — a gruff compliment which was taken advantage of by him when, after Fechter's début, he claimed the revolutionary *Séide as a pupil!*

At the end of three weeks Fechter left the Conservatoire, disgusted with a régime in which no two professors agreed.    Provost, Michelot, and Samson had removed the reverential veil from his eyes, and, losing respect for their judgment, he refused to submit to their instruction.    Disheartened, he discarded all thoughts of the stage, although he still memorized the classics and pursued his study of the French language with his old professor, Didier.    Putting his best energies into his night work at the Beaux Arts, he labored diligently for three years, and the summer of 1844 found him one of the graduating class competing for the first grand medal, which includes the high honor of being sent to Rome for five years at the expense of the government. Each scholar becomes a state's prisoner.    He is condemned to solitary confinement, with one hour's solitary exercise per day ; and at the end of six weeks, wet clay his only companion, is expected to take the form of a bas-relief of original composition.    The subject is always given and the best work obtains the prize. With emulation fully aroused, — anxious also to please his father, whose fondest hope was that his son should be a sculptor, — Fechter went to work with gusto upon the story of the Good Samaritan.    Making the composition as simple as possible, introducing the bare facts of two male figures and a donkey, Fechter saw in the classic dress an opportunity for the display of his knowledge of the human form, and took advantage of it. Finishing his task long before the expiration of the time specified, he was yet held in durance vile until the last moment, when he returned home to await the verdict of the examining committee.

Meanwhile Fechter's brother-in-law had been quietly working in an entirely different direction. Never forgetting his own and Fechter's passion for the stage, and believing that the lad was born for "only this and nothing more," Monsieur le Beau Frère inscribed Fechter's name on the list of applicants for débuts at the Théâtre Français. Any one is given this liberty; and if, after a test rehearsal, the applicant be deemed satisfactory, he is entitled to three public débuts, after which he is dismissed or received into the regular company, according to the ability displayed. Thus it happened that while Fechter was nervously awaiting the verdict of the Academy, he received an order to present himself before the tribunal of the Théâtre Français. Ignorant of the part played by his brother-in-law, and concluding that he had been called on the strength of merit only, he prepared himself as best he could. Trembling with fear he faced the unseen and unknown judges who sat before him, swallowed up in the darkness which reigns throughout the auditorium of a theatre by day. With a few footlights for inspiration, and Rachel's sister, Rebecca Félix, for prompter, Fechter began *Séide*, — the same rôle which he had rehearsed at the Conservatoire, and again selected because of its scope for the display of human

passions.   Slavery, religious fanaticism, and love make
up a character of flesh and blood very difficult to de-
lineate, but entirely in sympathy with a mind like Fechter's, that sought for nature in everything it attempted
to grasp.   Few of the French classical plays possess
the humanity of "Mahomet," and it is significant that
from the outset Fechter recognized the power of real
"situations."   Singularly enough Talma selected the
same rôle for his début, — a fact unknown to Fechter,
and therefore suggestive of rapport between the two
minds.

Fechter had not recited more than half of *Séide*
when a voice from out the darkness exclaimed, "That
will do; now for comedy."   Once more bracing himself to the task, he began the light-comedy part of
*Valère*, the lover in Molière's "Tartuffe."   Again, when
half-way through, the unknown voice broke the gloomy
silence with, "That will do; call another," — and Fechter bowed himself off the stage, utterly ignorant of the
effect produced upon the jury; but before leaving the
theatre he overheard the dismissal of his successor, a
woman, without any trial in comedy.   "At least I have
received better treatment than she," thought Fechter;
and laying this flattering unction to his soul he went
back to his studio in the Rue Paradis des Poisson-
nières.

Left in uncertainty, Fechter led a divided life between studying for the stage and modelling.   Racine,
Corneille, and Voltaire shared the honors with the
"Seven Capital Sins," — the subject he had selected
to put into clay.   These Capital Sins were to be rep-

resented around the same table, seated or otherwise, according to individual character, and carrying out the dominant passion in action and facial expression. Surely a good idea, but immensely difficult of treatment. It was because of its difficulty that Fechter selected the subject; and who can tell how great a sculptor posterity has lost?

Three months passed by, and, hearing nothing from the Théâtre Français, Fechter was again about to abandon the idea of acting, when a dragoon knocked at his door, and placed two official documents in his hands. The first announced the award by the Académie des Beaux Arts of the first grand medal; the second contained a call for Fechter's début at the Théâtre Français! No wonder that the youth of nineteen had an *accès de joie* at this embarrassment of riches. No wonder that Fechter *père* wellnigh danced with delight.

The prize had been won; would he go? "No, I cannot," said the son.

"You must," replied the father.

"It is impossible," answered the son. "My heart is wedded to the theatre."

The distress of Fechter *père* at this decision caused young Hotspur to relent so far as to offer to risk his future on a fencing-match with his father, the winner to decide whether it should be Rome or the stage.

"No, no," said his father, "I'll do no fencing, for at that you must surely win."

"Well, then, we'll toss up; heads I win, tails you lose."

To this the father consented. *Heads won*, and in December, 1844, Fechter made his début in conjunction with Rebecca Félix. The rôles were *Séide* and *Valère*, for which he had but one rehearsal. Rebecca Félix performed the part of *Palmire*.

From the beginning Fechter had ideas of his own; and, once convinced of having attained the truth in his art, no one could turn him from his purpose. The scene of Voltaire's " Mahomet " is laid in Mecca. *Séide, Mahomet's* slave, is an Arab, and should be dressed like an Arab, precedents to the contrary notwithstanding. So, armed with a fine Arab costume which hung in his studio, Fechter went to his dressing-room on the night of his début. There on a chair lay the properties supplied for *Séide* by the theatre, — blue and white satin, to contrast with the pink and white satin of *Palmire*, who, Arab as she ought to look, would be painted red and white, like the fairest of Circassians ! Stern in his resolve Fechter laid aside rouge, whiting, and satin, gave a dark olive tint to his complexion, donned his Arab costume, and went to the wings to await his cue.

" Mon Dieu ! what horror do I behold ? " screamed Geoffroy, the administrator of the week. " What do you mean by thus insulting established custom ? Off with the vile stuff ! Go to your room and put on the proper dress."

Flying from Geoffroy's rage Fechter, with no intention of obeying orders, retired under the stage, where he remained until sought for by the call-boy, when he rushed on to begin the second act, which is *Séide's* first appearance. A murmur ran through the audience, followed by a rustle which Fechter took for disapprobation. In an agony of doubt as to what would be the result of his temerity, he had almost lost his presence of mind, when a burst of applause and encouraging *bravos* assured him of sympathy before, if not behind, the curtain.

The real work of *Séide* begins with the fourth act, where, in the interview with *Palmire*, the slave he loves, not knowing her to be his sister, he reveals the dreadful oath he has taken to serve *Mahomet* by killing *Zopire* (his unknown father), to whom he is drawn by an unaccountable sympathy. This passionate dialogue, the appearance of *Zopire* kneeling at the altar of his gods, *Séide's* working himself up to the requisite amount of frenzy for the deed, and his return to *Palmire* after its accomplishment, wild in look and falling from exhaustion, as he exclaims,

> " Où suis-je ? et quelle voix m'appelle ?
> Je ne vois point Palmire ; un dieu m'a privé d'elle,"

were a revelation to the spectators of the Théâtre Français, who had been educated on declamation and propriety. Distracted and panting, *Séide* lay upon the ground, giving the question, " Qui, Zopire ? " in answer to that of *Palmire*, " Zopire, a-t-il perdu la vie ? " with a start and a heart-rending voice that thrilled the spectators.

> " Ah ! grand Dieu ! Dieu de sang altéré,
> Ne persécutez point son esprit égaré.
> Fuyons d'ici ! "

exclaims *Palmire.* Here *Séide* tried to rise, but falling on his knees,

"Je sens que mes genoux s'affaissent,"

delivered the confession of his crime, half reclining and
half kneeling, not regaining sufficient strength to stand
until the whole is told. No wonder that the public,
accustomed to see *Séide* obey Voltaire's printed " business " (*Il s'assied*), and *sit on a chair* in true Oriental
fashion, lost all sense of decorum, and actually called out
the real Arab at the end of this act. This was a rare
compliment for those days and never before known in
" Mahomet." No less effective was Fechter in the last
act, where, coming on delirious with poison administered unknown to him by *Mahomet's* orders, *Séide* calls
upon the people to avenge *Zopire's* death, denounces
*Mahomet*, and dies in the arms of his followers. Years
before, this scene had been cut out on account of its
difficulty, but Fechter had stomach for it all ; and, when
the curtain fell, his début was pronounced the success
of the night. Rachel came to him, saying " You must
act in my pieces ; I will play with nobody else."

Fechter selected *Valère* for his début in comedy,
because it gave him time to rest, *Valère* not appearing
until act second, and because it was short. There is
really only one good scene, quite enough however to
prove capacity, which was all that the occasion demanded. Again Fechter made a revolution in costume, wearing the dress of Louis the Fourteenth's time,
the scene of " Tartuffe " being laid in the Paris of *le
grand monarque.* Heretofore the costume had not

16. March 74.

Chère amie,

Stuart vient, à l'instant de me donner votre adresse que Madame S. S. m'avait remise en scène, au Lyceum, le soir de la dernière représentation, et qui fut égarée –

Je savais que c'était dans Grammercy Park et je m'y promenai une heure, le jour suivant esperant vous apercevoir mais en vain !

J'en fus absolument

désolé, ayant entendu
que je pourrais vous
être utile en quelque
chose.

Je n'ai pas besoin
de vous dire que vous
pouvez disposer de mon
affection; et que je suis
tout à vôtre service?

Faites donc état de
moi; et — si vous êtes
en ville — laissez moi
savoir, par un mot,
quelle est l'heure la
plus favorable pour
vous rendre visite; et
me mettre à vos ordres
Vôtre sincère:

210. East. 14th. Str.    Chas. Fechter
N. Y.

been strictly correct. The curtain fell upon a second success. Fechter had won his spurs in tragedy and comedy — in Voltaire and Molière — on the classic stage of the Théâtre Français, and had already gained Rachel's good will. Human nature is weak, artists are sadly jealous, and perhaps it is not strange that old *sociétaires* looked with ill favor upon the youth of nineteen who had jumped so suddenly into popularity. It was easy to reap a pitiful harvest of revenge; so the following week when Fechter went upon the stage to rehearse *Curiace* in Corneille's "Les Horaces" and *Dorante* in "Le Menteur," which parts he had chosen for his second début, he found himself without support. Righteously indignant at this unseemly slight, Fechter left word that he would act in neither piece, and the manager might get somebody else. Later entreaty availed naught; old *sociétaires* assumed their old rôles and the début was postponed another week.

What said Jules Janin, the prince of dramatic critics, the man who could not be bought with money, but who revenged himself upon such artists as did not pay him court? "Bravo! bravissimo!" murmured Janin in private; "come and see me, Fechter." Quixotically independent and indifferent to the verdict of critics, Fechter offended Janin's *amour propre* by staying away. So the *feuilleton* that followed the representations of "Les Horaces" and "Le Menteur," in both of which Fechter was supposed to have appeared, but which he threw up as has already been told, contained a most savage onslaught upon Fechter's *Curiace* and *Dorante*. The actor had his critic com-

pletely on the hip, but took no further advantage than
to write the following private note : —

"DEAR JANIN, — Your criticism is excellent : true
in every particular, except in attributing the acting of
*Curiace* and *Dorante* to me. *I performed in neither
part !*"

In the next week's *feuilleton* the impartial critic
stated that, owing to gross carelessness, his manuscript
had been misprinted.    His remarks àpropos of Mr.
Fechter were intended for his rehearsal, and *not* for
the performance, in which other artists had appeared.
It was quite evident from this second falsehood that
Janin meant war to the knife ; so Fechter returned the
blow by publicly stating that, inasmuch as he had never
rehearsed the parts criticised by M. Jules Janin, the
explanation of the latter could hardly be called satisfactory !    After this terrible and justifiable *exposé*, what
was left for Janin but silence ?    And silence was his
enduring revenge.    Even after Fechter's marvellous
success in "La Dame aux Camélias " Janin made but a
passing notice of his name, which was recorded among
the supernumeraries.    In Paris, as well as in America,
personality degrades art.

The young *Séide* had not been three weeks a *pensionnaire* at the Théâtre Français before he broke an
audacious lance in behalf of republican institutions.
Entering the green-room for the first time, he saw
all the *sociétaires* ranged on one side of the fireplace
and the *pensionnaires* on the other.    The former re-

ceived their appointment originally from the first Napoleon, who accorded to the Théâtre Français a yearly subvention of sixteen thousand pounds sterling. Since then *sociétaires* have been elected by their own body. They divide the profits of the theatre among themselves, — at the end of twenty years can retire on a pension of five thousand dollars, or, remaining longer in the profession, are entitled to a still larger pension. Thus does France foster art. *Sociétaires* consequently hold the reins in their own hands ; while *pensionnaires*, being on a salary and lower in official grade, are made to feel the difference between the throne and the step leading to it. "What's the meaning of this?" asked Fechter. "Why are all the *sociétaires* in one row and the *pensionnaires* in another? Is there no equality among artists?" With this the young democrat sprang from one side of the wide fireplace to the other and, landing among the *sociétaires*, began talking to Beauvallet as if nothing unusual had occurred, and as if *pensionnaires* had a right to trespass upon sacred ground.

Fechter's second débuts, when he appeared in "Les Horaces" with Rachel, and in "Le Menteur," were received with plaudits. In the comedy Fechter again taught actors and public a lesson by wearing a thoroughly correct Charles-the-Second dress. So pronounced was the success that then and there Fechter became a regular member of the Théâtre Français, the high powers not deeming it necessary to await his third débuts. La Rue being lazy and Maillard ill, Fechter at first had many opportunities of testing his ability.   Rachel's desires were fulfilled, and she found wonderful support in the stripling who, ignoring precedents, made human beings of *Hippolyte, Oreste, Xiphares, Bajazet,* and *Nérestan.*   It was at the conclusion of "Zaire" that Regnier came behind the scenes and, addressing the assembled *sociétaires,* exclaimed " Now mark my words.   I tell you that he is better than any of you."   Such outspoken criticism was not likely to promote the interests of a beginner who was himself none too politic.   Moreover Buloz had private reasons for advancing a vastly inferior actor, and Fechter was soon made to feel the difference between favoritism and real worth.   Appearing in the comedies of "Valérie," "Les Femmes Savantes," "Les Précieuses Ridicules," "Le Dépit," "Le Ménage Parisien," "Le Misanthrope," "Tartuffe," "Les Fourberies de Scapin," and "La Vestale," he at last found himself shorn of almost every part rightfully his own. Notwithstanding that Dumas *père* wrote the prominent male character in "La Fille du Régent" for Fechter, and spoke of having done so, when the play came to be cast Fechter found a part in the prologue assigned to him.   Easy in his principles, Dumas had been talked over by Buloz and others.

Though Fechter had a right to a third début with his own selection of parts, though it is a rule that every débutant shall perform the parts of every début at least twice during his first year, or whenever the plays are brought out, these rights were denied.   Fechter felt that the *sociétaires* never intended to give him fair play ; and when, at the beginning of 1846, the salary of every *pensionnaire* except himself was raised, the intention could not be mistaken. After appealing in vain for justice Fechter frankly avowed his opinion, and at the end of eighteen months left the theatre in a glory of indignation. A man of less spirit and more phlegm might have known better how to subvert the machinations of rivals; but in all probability a man of less spirit would not have been so good an actor, and therefore could not have fared so ill. Extraordinary ability is a dangerous possession, unless it be master of the situation and be tempered with wisdom. Wisdom and Fechter were never boon companions. Thus closed Fechter's career at the Théâtre Français.

With illusions gone, with aspirations clouded, Fechter returned to his studio for the fourth time, and betook himself to modelling. Once more he went to work upon the Seven Capital Sins, and it is safe to conclude that he put a great deal of devilish expression into the face of Envy. " Theatres ! " he said ; " never say Theatre to me. I 've done with the stage. Henceforth I am a sculptor." And so the actor believed ; but Fate knew better. One day it chanced — as it always chances, in life as well as in books — that Dacier, the celebrated baritone, brought St. Aubin, once leading actor at the Gymnase and then manager of the Berlin Theatre Royal, to Fechter's studio for the purpose of seeing his statue. " By the way," said St. Aubin, " are you related to Fechter of the Théâtre Français, about whom I 've heard so much? "

" Well, rather," replied the sculptor ; " I am that identical individual."

" Is it possible ?   Then how is it that you are at work here ? "

" For the reason that I have renounced the stage. I shall never act again."

" What, you? the most promising man of the day? This will never do.   Come with me to Berlin.   I am forming a company for the Theatre Royal; you shall have just the parts you like, and as you will be paid by the government, you need have no fear on the score of money."

Fechter accepted this offer ; the Seven Capital Sins were once more wrapped in wet cloths, and with the agility of Harlequin the sculptor transformed himself into an actor.   There was nothing that Fechter did not do in Berlin.   He was everything by turns and nothing long.   He was the best actor in the troupe " either for tragedy, comedy, history, pastoral, pastoral-comical, historical-comical, scene individable, or poem unlimited."   He had a fine robust tenor voice, and sang, entirely by ear, the music of *Daniel* in the opera of " Le Chalet."   He played Paul Taglioni's ballet of " Le Corsair," and executed the dances with admirable effect.   He made a great success as *Le Père Turlultutu*, in " One Hundred Years Old," and still another in doubling *Buckingham* and *Tyrrell* in " Les Enfants d'Edouard," a piece taken from Shakespeare's " Richard III."   Fechter was so entirely transformed in the second assumption that the public failed to recognize him until the end of the act.

Being a very devout Catholic the Queen abstained from theatrical performances, but after repeated entreaty from the King, with whom Fechter was a great favorite, she consented to assist at a court representation at Potsdam of Bayard and Mélesville's comedy "Le Chevalier de St. George," and Dupin's "La Polka en Province." Reaching high-water mark, Fechter delighted the court. In the afterpiece Fechter's comedy was so inimitable that the King sent his chamberlain behind the scenes to request him to be less funny, — otherwise his Majesty would die. Misunderstanding the message, and seeing that the King enjoyed the performance, Fechter became more and more comical, until royalty degenerated into base humanity and was carried out of his box in a state of exhaustion from laughing. The Queen expressed her admiration in an autograph letter, accompanied by busts of Schiller, Goethe, and Herder. Not to be outdone, Fechter modelled a Sister of Charity kneeling at prayer, and sent it to the Queen, who placed the artist's gift in the Royal Gallery, where it still remains.

After an unusually prolonged and successful season of nine months Fechter returned to Paris in 1847, and immediately signed an engagement for three years at the Vaudeville, where he looked forward to a reign of peace. The manager was all grace, the public all smiles ; and his rendering of the hero *Albert* in " Marguérite " received the approving nod of claque and critics. About two weeks after its production the manager went to Fechter and with simulated enthusiasm exclaimed : " My dear fellow, your performance was admirable. You are the only man to replace Frederic Lemaître. I must make another engagement with you.

The present one is not equal to your merits.   Give me the old contract, and I 'll have a better one made out." Dumfounded at this excess of virtue, and not suspecting foul play, Fechter complied with the request. However, after waiting a reasonable time and waiting in vain, he ventured to ask for the new contract.   Mr. Manager coolly ignored it.   An unworthy power behind the managerial desk had instigated the treachery and caused the written articles to be destroyed.

Stung to the quick by this baseness, and able to produce witnesses to the existence of a contract, Fechter had about decided to go to law, when he met an old artist friend, Anthony Beraud, who was manager of the Ambigu.   "Why, what 's the matter, Fechter?" inquired the latter ;  "you look upset."

"Upset ! I should rather think I was."   And then followed a narration of what had occurred.

"Now take my advice," said the manager, at the conclusion of the woful story.   "Don't go to law, but come to my theatre.   I 'll double your present salary, and bind myself by more writing than you 'll care to read."

"Agreed," cried Fechter ; and the threatening clouds disappeared.

Prior to this engagement Fechter went to London with a troupe of admirable artists, including Boccage, Cartigny, Montalent, Josset, Mademoiselle Baptiste (granddaughter of the great Baptiste), and others. The season at the St. James's lasted four months, during which time Fechter appeared in standard plays, the most prominent being Sophocles's "Antigone."   It was brought out with great care, and excited unusual attention. The Queen and Prince Consort were constant in their attendance, not being absent more than twenty nights. D'Orsay was seen constantly, and with him Louis Napoleon, who made Fechter's acquaintance and often went behind the scenes to compliment his countryman. Upon bidding Fechter goodby Napoleon seemed much touched at the thought of his own continued exile from France, and said, "The next time we meet will be in the Tuileries."

"That is somewhat doubtful," answered Fechter, "for I really do not intend to be King."

"*No*," replied the man of destiny, "*but I intend to be Emperor!*"

To smile was impossible. Napoleon's tone and manner were such as to convince Fechter that an oracle had spoken, and when the Prince became President of the Republic, Fechter knew how the drama would end. Napoleon was right. The next time they met was in the Tuileries, and when Fechter acted at Fontainebleau, the Emperor took off his watch and chain and begged the artist's acceptance of them.

Fechter made so strong an impression in London that Maddox, manager of the Princess's, went to him with an offer of forty pounds per week for three years if he would appear on the English stage. This was a large salary for those days and the young artist felt greatly inclined to accept it, but there rose before him the promise to his friend of the Ambigu. He wrote to be released, if release were possible. "Impossible," was the reply. "Sue and others are writing plays for you, and I cannot let you go." So toward the end of February, 1848, Fechter returned to Paris with the expectation of fulfilling this engagement, making his *entrée* in a new play, " La Famille Thureau," the first and only production of an eccentric painter, Lorentz. During the performance of " La Famille Thureau," the story of which is not unlike that of " La Dame aux Camélias," Fechter, while engaged in a dialogue of twelve or fifteen minutes, modelled a statue of Poetry, three feet high. Fair as the prospect was, it did not long continue. A Revolution came between him and public attention ; and as the real drama surpassed in interest any that could be feigned, the Ambigu, following the example of other theatres, closed after a season of twelve nights. Freed from obligations Fechter wrote to Maddox, accepting his former offer, but the letter arrived too late. The enterprising manager had already engaged an opera troupe, which absorbed his time and money.

*Othello's* occupation gone, Fechter solaced himself with fencing and shooting. In those days of anarchy no man knew what destiny lay in wait for him, and discretion led to anticipation of the worst. So Fechter fenced and fired himself into an enviable notoriety. No one dared to quarrel with him, lest a duel might be the consequence. Rochefort always referred to him with deference, and bullies gave him a wide berth. While Fechter was thus vigorously engaged Adrien Decourcelles went to him, saying, " I 've just written a reactionary play called ' Oscar XXVIII.,' which if possible I want to have performed. You are the only man who has pluck enough to brave the crowd. I 've burlesqued the Revolution. I anticipate what will most certainly happen months hence ; and if you and I can show the people themselves, as they are and must be, it will be a great feather in our caps." Fechter read the play, sympathized with the travesty of royalty on the one side and mad democracy on the other, and with his usual daring consented to play " Oscar XXVIII." The next step was to secure a theatre, and they appealed to Moran of the Variétés.

" But you 'll have the theatre down," argued the timid manager.

" Yes, that 's one side of the argument," replied author and actor ; " but, on the other hand, you *may* make a great deal of money. Your theatre is closed. Here is an opportunity of turning an ill wind to good account. If you don't seize it, some other theatre will."

Persuaded in spite of himself, Moran consented to the production of " Oscar XXVIII." On the first night none but members of the press were present ; nevertheless, Moran could not be found. Anticipating trouble he had left Fechter and Decourcelles to bear the onus of it, instead of which they received the plaudits of a non-paying but appreciative audience.

A few hours acquainted Paris with the nature of the entertainment, and for two months, during the turbulent summer of 1848, " Oscar XXVIII." laughed in the face of the Revolution, and drew crowded audiences of reactionists. Instead of assaults upon the actors, there were occasional combats among the spectators, at which times Fechter delivered impromptu addresses upon the folly of useless expenditure of force in the presence of a play brought out for the express purpose of putting the people on exhibition. "Only keep the peace and we'll show you just how it ought to be done," said Fechter; and, taken aback by his audacity and wit, the combatants were wont to sit down and look at their own portraits. Nine months later the burlesque of "Oscar XXVIII." became a positive reality. Decourcelles and Fechter had merely anticipated history.

Later in this year Fechter fulfilled an engagement at the Théâtre Historique, performing Dumas's rhymed tragedy of "Charles VII.," his drama of "Angèle," and bringing out for the first time Dumas and Maquet's "Catilina," and Paul Féval's "Mystères de Londres."

1849 found him again at the Ambigu, during which twelve months he created no less than seven characters of totally different types, the pieces being Fournier's "Pardon de Bretagne," Paul Féval's "Mauvais Cœur," Charles Desnoyer's comedy of "Les Trois Etages," Léon Gozlan's "Jeunesse Dorée," Masson's "Les Fils Aymon," Bourgeois's "Notre Dame de Paris," and Labrousse's "Louis the Fourteenth." In the last, Fechter, in the hero who attempts to save the *Queen*, assumed seven different characters and surprised the audience by his wonderful "make-ups," being especially effective as a cab-driver. When the "Courier of Lyons" was brought out at the Gaieté a year later,

Paulin Menier made an exact copy of Fechter's cab-driver, and gained a success thereby.

1850 and 1851 were equally divided between the Théâtre Historique and the Porte-Saint-Martin. In this time Dumas's " Pauline " and " Corsican Brothers," Bulwer's " Money," Émile Souvestre's " Le Lion et le Moucheron," De Montépin's " Le Vol à la Duchesse," George Sand's " Claudie," and Thiboust's " Le Diable " were first put upon the stage. The " Corsican Brothers " ran for one hundred nights ; while " Money," though pronounced a great artistic success, only held the stage forty nights. It was too high comedy for a melodramatic theatre. " Claudie," at the Porte-Saint-Martin, rivalled the " Corsican Brothers " in the length of its popularity, whereby " hangs a tale." When the drama was first read Boccage, to whom belonged the leading rôle, that of an old man, went to Fechter saying, " We can offer you nothing in ' Claudie,' as I have the first part, and no other is good enough for you."

" On the contrary," rejoined Fechter, " I have taken a fancy to the ploughboy."

" What, the third part in the piece ? "

" Never mind, we 'll see what can be made of it."

So " Claudie " was mounted, and Madame Sand came from Nohant to assist at the dress rehearsal. At the end of the first act Fechter overheard an excited dialogue between Madame Sand and Boccage in the dressing-room adjoining his own.

" It will kill ' Claudie,' " said Madame Sand. " I will not permit such an outrage. If you allow that man to act I 'll withdraw the play."

"But, my dear madame," retorted Boccage, "you don't know what you are talking about. That man, as you call him, is doing you a great honor. He has taken an inferior part out of compliment to you, and will act it as no one else can. My advice to you is to keep quiet."

But Madame Sand turned a deaf ear to this advice, and with threats upon her lips left Boccage to his own reflections.

"What's the matter, Boccage?" asked Fechter, as soon as the lady had retired.

"Why, that foolish woman says you sha'n't play in 'Claudie.' She's made a ploughboy, and is very much disgusted with you because you dress him in peasant's clothes and give him a *patois.*"

"Very well," answered Fechter, "then *I* refuse the part. I won't go on with the rehearsal."

"But we are lost if you don't. For my sake, pay no attention to her, and go through your part."

Gradually soothed into complaisance, Fechter put on his street dress, spoke the purest of French, and at the close of the next act Madame Sand exclaimed: "What a charming young man! Why did he not look and act this way before?"

Fechter had made a gentleman of her ploughboy.

"Now," said Fechter, at the conclusion of the rehearsal, "if I can't do that part as I feel it ought to be done, I won't appear at all. Madame Sand can write, but she has proved that she doesn't know the meaning of acting. She has insulted me, and I've done with her."

Of course much expostulation ensued, and it was finally decided that, Madame Sand to the contrary notwithstanding, Fechter should have his own way, by which he made *the* success of the play. "Take me to him," exclaimed Madame Sand when the curtain fell upon the first night of "Claudie," — "take me to him, that I may know him."

" I refuse to know Madame Sand," was Fechter's answer to this message. "You need not bring her. I do not forget an insult."

Madame Sand did not obtain her introduction ; and when she wrote "Mauprat" especially for the man whom she declared would kill "Claudie," the foolishly proud actor refused to accept his part.

The production of "Le Diable" being assigned to Fechter, he designed the dresses, read the play to the actors, superintended the rehearsals, and brought it ont five days after receiving the manuscript. It was at this theatre also that Fechter gave up thirty thousand francs of salary to minor actors who were suffering in consequence of the manager's failure during the engagement of another artist.

The next six years — from 1852 to 1858 — Fechter was the star of the Vaudeville, where ten new plays were produced in which he personated the hero. These creations were Gozlan's " Le Coucher d'une Étoile " and " Louise de Nauteuil," Bayard's " Hortense de Ceruy " and " Les Contes de Boccace," Dumas's " La Dame aux Camélias," Barrière's " Les Filles de Marbre," " La Vie en Rose," and " On Demande un Gouverneur," Scribe's " La Fille de Trente Ans," and

Maquet's " Les Dettes de Cœur." Successful in all, Fechter made a great impression in a very difficult rôle in " Hortense de Ceruy." This, however, was eclipsed by the furore he created in " La Dame aux Camélias." Fechter objected to the fourth act of this play as originally written, and suggested certain changes of situation and dialogue, to which Dumas at first willingly assented, but over which he grew exceedingly nervous as the trial night approached.

" If my play is a failure I 'll lay the blame on you," said Dumas to Fechter.

" Nous verrons," responded the actor.

The curtain went up, the curtain went down, and the fourth act was over. " What mean that noise and tremendous applause ? " asked Fechter of himself. " Is it a failure ? Is it disapprobation ? "

"Fechter, Fechter, you have made a sensation ; you are called ! " And the Vaudeville witnessed an expression of unexampled enthusiasm. The *chef* of the claque came behind the scenes, in great trepidation. " It was n't I ! " he cried. " It was not my doing. The people did it, tell the manager. I tried to keep applause back for the last act, but they would have their own way." Dumas hurried to Fechter and clasped him in his arms ; while Madame Doche, who had had nothing to do with the sensation of this act, clever as she was in what followed, calmly remarked : " Ah oui. Il m'a bien secondé ! "

This play ran for upwards of three hundred nights, and whether Doche, Jeanne Essler, or others personated the heroine, the success, with Fechter as *Armand,*

was equally great. What Dumas thought, all who read
may learn : —

"Thanks to Fechter. What can I say of him that
all the world does not say and know? Fechter is the
most youthful, most ardent, most enthusiastic, most
insinuating of artists. What variety of talents, what
unpretending skill in conception, what marvellous,
thrilling, electric execution ! Be it in 'Mauvais
Cœur' at the Ambigu, in the 'Corsican Brothers' at
the Théâtre Historique, in 'Claudie' at the Porte-
Saint-Martin, in 'Hortense de Ceruy' or in 'La
Dame aux Camélias' at the Vaudeville, he is always
the character *first ;* then those happy, unexpected in-
spirations which are the seal of great artists, which
transport an entire audience at once, and invest the
character with charms and proportions that the author
himself, with all his high ambition, never dreamed of.
In 'La Dame aux Camélias' the illusion is complete.
It is not an actor playing ; it is the man taken in the
very act. Fechter has the action, the look, the voice
of our inmost emotions, of our most frequent passions.
He is himself; he is ourselves. For a drama in which
I have endeavored to cause the footlights to disappear
and to bring the spectator in direct communication
with its characters, for this study in which I have
wished that a generation might live over even its errors,
where could I have found a surer accomplice than
Fechter, young in years, mature in talent? I am
happy ; it is but my duty to avow it. I seek, I ask in
vain : who could have given to *Armand Duval* the con-
vincing poetry, the noble jealousy, the indescribable

susceptibilities of feeling, — the naturalness, the terror — with which he shaded the first three acts? As for the frenzy of the fourth, at the end of which the entire audience rose to cheer and to recall him, — him and Madame Doche, — if I were not so satisfied at having written the piece, I should wish some one else to have been its author that I might say of Fechter all that ought to be said. His heart beat in every part of the theatre. In the fifth act he gave the most piercing cry of which human grief is capable. Happy the brother author who next has Fechter for his hero ! Happy I, who, taking my turn in representing the public, shall go to hear him and to clap my hands ! "

Did ever actor receive greater praise from dramatist? And well might Dumas applaud, — he who had done all for the heroine, making *Armand* a secondary figure and expecting no more from him than is down in the book ! It is cleverness that succeeds in doing well what the author has made pre-eminent; it is genius that carries the author's conception beyond the letter, and makes the less appear the greater. After seeing Fechter in *Armand*, Lemaître went to him, saying : "You are a great fool, my dear fellow. You throw yourself away. You always do justice to every portion of your rôle. Your performance is so even, so good throughout, that the audience does n't appreciate you half as much as it ought. Now take my advice ; follow my example. Save yourself for your great points, and the people will be so startled by the strong contrast as to go quite wild. Don't you do anything in *Armand* until the fourth act, and then you 'll see a hurricane of enthusiasm." But Fechter refused to take Lemaître's advice. He was too true an artist to play for effects; and the great Frederic left him with the final remark that of all fools he was the biggest.

Looking back upon " La Dame aux Camélias," it is interesting to know that, though rehearsed on the stage of the Conservatoire during the Revolution, the moral censors of the Republic would not consent to its production; and not until the days of the Empire did Dumas's masterpiece receive gracious treatment. Count Morny attended the first rehearsal expecting to be greatly shocked. "What fools those Republicans were!" he muttered, and immediately withdrew every objection.

Simultaneously with Scribe's "La Fille de Trente Ans" came Sardou's "Pattes de Mouche." "Which shall we accept?" asked the manager.

"'Pattes de Mouche,' by all means," said Fechter. "It is admirable. Scribe's play will fail, in spite of acting." When Scribe heard the verdict he went to Fechter and upbraided him. "Say no more about it," replied Fechter. "It was policy, not friendship, that prompted my decision. As a friend I will do anything for you, Scribe. Your comedy shall be accepted."

It was produced; it failed. The theatre was saved by a revival of "La Dame aux Camélias;" and Sardou's "Pattes de Mouche" fulfilled Fechter's predictions by running one hundred and fifty nights at the Gymnase.

In "Les Contes de Boccace," a five-act comedy, Fechter sustained no less than nine characters; while in "La Vie en Rose" he became the hero of a lawsuit as well as of the play. Not having read the piece before its acceptance by the manager, Fechter declared that he would not perform in it unless the last two acts were entirely changed. He would not be connected with another failure. The parts had been given out, the date of production announced, and the manager in despair resorted to law. Law, however, did not produce the desired effect, as the verdict accorded three months' grace to Fechter, after which he was expected to comply with the manager's demands. Fechter asked for no better terms, as it only needed delay to kill the obnoxious play. Completely at Fechter's mercy, the manager went to him, saying, —

"Dictate your own terms. Barrière is down stairs in a hack. He will do anything you please, provided you 'll play in his piece immediately."

"Very well," responded Fechter; "let him alter those two acts as at first suggested, and I 'll rehearse."

Thus, while the company rehearsed the first three acts, Barrière reconstructed the last two, and " La Vie en Rose " had a rose-colored reception from the public.

One night, during the performance of the comedy " On Demande un Gouverneur," Fechter was greatly inconvenienced by talking that proceeded from a stage-box. Nothing so embarrasses or mortifies an artist as this most brutal of insults, and nothing so justifies resentment. Louder and louder grew the noise until, in righteous exasperation, Fechter impulsively flung his cane into the box with such force that it whizzed like a bullet. He then coolly rang a bell, and ordered the astonished servant to stop the noise and fetch him his cane. A dead silence took possession of the previously boisterous spectators; and a cold shiver passed over the rest of the audience, who saw in this act a speedy challenge, followed by a duel and the possible death of one of the combatants. "Fechter's done it again," whispered those of his friends who knew his readiness to resent injustice and insult; and Fechter himself was quite prepared for the worst, so that when the card of M. le Comte —— was sent to him in his dressing-room, he expected to be called out.

"Monsieur Fechter," said M. le Comte, upon entering the dressing-room. "I owe you a very humble apology for my conduct. A short time ago I was intoxicated and insulted you unconsciously. Your cane brought me to my senses, and I now come to you for pardon."

Of course Fechter's wrath was quickly appeased, and M. le Comte took his departure with protestations of everlasting friendship upon his lips.

Leaving the Vaudeville Fechter made a successful tour through the provinces, ending with Lyons, where he was to give six representations of "La Dame aux Camélias." Hisses greeted his first appearance, the Lyonnais having given their allegiance to another actor in *Armand*, and being determined to make Lyons thoroughly uncomfortable for Fechter. "Ladies and gentlemen," said Fechter, approaching the footlights, "it makes no possible difference whether you like or dislike me, whether I act or do not act; I merely wish to say that, if I hear another hiss, I shall leave the theatre and never enter it again."

Silenced by this independence the Lyonnais kept their madness in the background, but preserved a discouraging gloom until the end of the fourth act, when Fechter's passion broke down their prejudice, and former enemies became ardent admirers. Before Fechter bade farewell to Lyons his six nights had lengthened into three months.

Returning to Paris Fechter accepted a profitable engagement at the Porte-Saint-Martin, where at the end of ten months, after having appeared in two new parts — in Ségour's " Fils de Nuit," and Maquet's " Belle Gabrielle " — his engagement was cut short by a dangerous attack of typhoid fever which seized him suddenly while acting. Singularly enough he had but just climbed a wall, and been fired upon from below by an actor who was supposed to be pursuing him, when he fell upon the stage as if he had been shot. A short time before, an actor at the same theatre had barely escaped death, owing to the pistol being loaded ; and imagining a similar accident, Fechter's fellow-player startled the audience by crying out, " I have killed him ! " but afterwards pacified the excited multitude by assuring them there was no wound. For five months Fechter did not leave his bed ; nor was he able to resume his profession until seven months later. Overwork had brought on disease, and rest was his only salvation. During the last five months of his stay at the Porte-Saint-Martin he had rehearsed pieces for the Odéon, the management of which he was about to assume. Exhausted Nature took her revenge. Upon recovery Fechter carried out this intention and, before himself

reappearing, mounted "André Gerard" for Frederic
Lemaître. He made his *rentrée* in Ponsard's "L'Hon-
neur et l'Argent."

Loving the art of acting quite as much if not more
than his own personal advancement, Fechter assumed
the management of the Odéon with the intention of
producing standard plays in a manner heretofore unknown. Racine, Corneille, Voltaire, Molière, and
Beaumarchais were to be humanized for the first time.
Rhyme and hexameter were to be given colloquially.
History was to be respected in *mise en scène* and
costume. Turks were not to sit on French upholstery,
nor was imperial Rome to be longer shorn of its splendor of appointments. If the *sociétaires* of the Théâtre
Français were content to violate the laws of eternal fitness, at least Fechter aspired to better things. Such
audacity filled the *sociétaires* with anger and dismay.
"What! a minor theatre dare to produce our pieces,
and in a style superior to ourselves? We will show
Fechter our superiority."

So when Fechter brought out "Tartuffe," he playing
*Tartuffe* for the first time, the same comedy was announced at the Théâtre Français. It would be given
three nights a week until the freebooter of the Odéon
was sufficiently punished; but the public failed to
appreciate this consideration, and the irate *sociétaires*
were obliged to withdraw "Tartuffe" after the second
night. Not so Fechter. His interpretation of the entire comedy was a revelation to playgoers. Night after
night found Meissonnier at the theatre, making sketches
of the costumes and scenery. "Il a mis 'Tartuffe'

dans ses meubles," said the journals. Fould, Minister of State, wrote to Fechter, expressing his delight and declaring that he enjoyed it with all the relish of a new play. But Fould was first a servant of the government, then a man ; and when the sacred powers of the sacred Théâtre Français demonstrated to him the impropriety of Fechter's poaching upon their ground, Fould requested the withdrawal of " Tartuffe." " No," replied Fechter, " I cannot. A success of thirty nights proves that my efforts in behalf of dramatic art are appreciated by the public. When the sun of 'Tartuffe' sets, that of 'Britannicus' will rise with equal splendor." And he meant what he said. While acting in two new plays, " Le Rocher de Sysiphe " and Emile Augier's " La Jeunesse," " Britannicus," and " Macbeth " were receiving the most elaborate and careful rehearsals. When Fechter closed his first season of nine months, he determined that his reopening should mark an era in dramatic art.

Going to England during the summer of 1860 for the purpose of regaining his health, Fechter received flattering offers from Harris, who had superseded Maddox in the management of the Princess's ; but all aglow with the idea of bringing out French and English classics in his own language, he refused to be tempted. Then, going to the Tuileries, he applied to the Emperor for what is called *la liberté des théâtres*, — that is, the right to perform such plays as had heretofore been the exclusive property of the Théâtre Français. Receiving Fechter with cordiality, Napoleon declared that, if his own consent were alone required, the despotic law should be immediately rescinded. Unfortunately he could only recommend its annulment to the Chamber of Deputies, and this he would do most gladly. For once the Chamber of Deputies failed to agree with their imperial master; and Fechter impulsively bade farewell to the Paris he loved so well, declared he had no intention of devoting his life to melodrama, and crossed over to England. Had he waited patiently his dream would have been realized, for Napoleon never forgot Fechter's request, and two years later brought about the necessary reform. " Come back," said the Emperor; but the battle had been fought and Fechter could not resign his victory. He had conquered a foreign tongue and a foreign audience, and would not leave Shakespeare for Racine.

Understanding English perfectly when spoken, Fechter flattered himself that it would cost little effort to speak it equally well; but the mystified *What ?* of the cabman, to whom he gave directions upon arriving in London, convinced the voluntary exile that there was no royal road to Shakespeare. Devoting himself for four months to our stern Anglo-Saxon language, he studied sixteen and eighteen hours out of the twenty-four.

Selecting " Ruy Blas," which had never been acted in English, as less likely to display his deficiencies of pronunciation than a native play, Fechter made his début at the Princess's Theatre on the 27th of October, 1860. The novelty of seeing an eminent French actor translated into English created more than a momentary sensation. The papers were enthusiastic, and *Ruy Blas* became the hero of a hundred nights. Not yet daring to trust himself with classical language, Fechter's next venture was in the "Corsican Brothers;" after which, feeling more glib with his tongue, he made his comedy entrée on February 11, 1861, in "Don Cæsar de Bazan." Six weeks later, the date being March 20, he first essayed *Hamlet*. It was aiming high, but not higher than he could attain. Courage is the friendly breeze that ever fills the sails of genius; and Fechter, long familiar with Shakespeare, did not feel as if he were undertaking anything new. His conception of *Hamlet* was so thoroughly original that it became the *open-sesame* to conversation in households and clubs. The actor was transformed into a lion, — members of the royal family, the aristocracy and gentry rivalling one another in offers of hospitality.

"Perhaps," wrote Charles Dickens, "no innovation in art was ever accepted with so much favor by so many intellectual persons, precommitted to and pre-occupied by another system, as Mr. Fechter's *Hamlet*." There were those who exclaimed, as they exclaim in America, "C'est magnifique, mais ce n'est pas la guerre," but he had powerful support from the best minds. It was after seeing Fechter in *Hamlet* that Dickens sought an introduction, which took place at a dinner given by Chorley, the musical critic, and which led to a lasting friendship. So great an impression did Fechter make, that "Hamlet" continued running for one hundred and fifteen nights, from the 20th of March until the end of August! For twenty-one nights it was acted six times in the week; but the strain being too great on Fechter, who felt his text most acutely, it was limited to four nights a week.

"Mr. Fechter," declared that captious critic the *Saturday Review* "is a most logical actor. With all his intention to be original and unfettered, he does not deviate from the prescribed path without warrant from the text, or at any rate, without full conviction that there is nothing in the text that can be opposed to his innovations."

"Mr. Fechter does not act; he *is Hamlet*," asserted the *Athenæum;* while G. H. Lewes, who rarely praised any acting, admitted that Fechter's conception was "fine," "consonant in general with what the text of Shakespeare indicates." In Lewes's book on "Actors and Acting" we read that "Fechter is lymphatic, delicate, handsome; and, with his long flaxen curls, quivering sensitive nostrils, fine eye and sympathetic voice, perfectly represents the graceful *Prince*. His aspect and bearing are such that the eye rests on him with delight. Our sympathies are completely secured."

Taking a vacation of two months, Fechter reappeared, on the 23d of October, in "Othello." Here was another hard nut for the critics to crack, and the war of *pro* and *con* waxed fierce and loud. Fechter's *Othello* was his own, and for forty nights the theatre overflowed with deeply curious and deeply interested audiences.

On the night of his début in the "Moor of Venice" Fechter's acting edition of the tragedy was widely circulated. In his dedication to Richard Lane, Esq., Fechter declared the convictions that were in him.

He avowed his firm belief that Shakespeare's plays were certainly written to be *acted* not *recited*, and that his conclusions were the fruit of nearly twenty years' unceasing labor of love for the *scenic* representation of the Great Master. After expressing his disregard of Tradition, Fechter presented his views of how "Othello" should be acted. Elaborate stage directions supplemented the text and gave a precise idea of the actor's intentions.

These intentions were not received with general favor. "His *Hamlet* was one of the very best and his *Othello* one of the very worst I have ever seen," wrote the uncompromising Lewes. "On leaving the theatre after 'Hamlet,' I felt once more what a great play it was, with all its faults, and they are gross and numerous. On leaving the theatre after 'Othello,' I felt as if all my old admiration for this supreme masterpiece of the art had been an exaggeration."

For years there had been no such excitement over legitimate drama as this Gallic *Othello* created, — an excitement, however, that was cut short by the approach of the pantomime season.[1] Fechter refused to act in conjunction with *Columbine* and *Harlequin*, retired from the theatre, and left Mr. Harris to ruminate on the fallibility of managerial judgment ; for, in accordance with Fechter's predictions, the public that had applauded Shakespeare failed to recognize the superiority of his successors.

"Come back," implored Mr. Harris at the close of the third week.

[1] For Press Criticisms, see page 177.

"No, I am not a feather to be blown about at will,"
replied Fechter. "You said you would run your pantomime ten weeks, and run it you may. When I
return, it will be to perform *Iago* and not *Othello*."

Mr. Harris did not love Fechter for thus paying him
in his own coin, — human nature never enjoys retorts
of this description, — but being helpless, submitted to
the actor's terms and gathered a rich harvest in consequence. *Iago* attracted large audiences for several
weeks. Then Fechter brought out "The Golden Daggers," a drama taken by himself from Paul Féval's
novel of the same name, the scene being laid in Mex-
ico. Admirably as the drama was acted, and beautifully as it was put upon the stage, it failed to be a
pecuniary success. A modern story, and perfectly
quiet natural acting, disappointed the general public.
"There's no use in going to see that," they said; "it's
just what people do at home."

So "Hamlet" was revived. At this time Fechter
received a fine offer from Ullman to visit the United
States; but not wishing to leave England during the
great Exhibition, when he expected to continue acting
at the Princess's, he declined. Then came Harris's revenge. Fechter had dared to dictate to him, and would
not perform "Hamlet" more than four nights in the
week. London would teem with people; the theatre
would be patronized, no matter what the attraction.
Fechter should be sacrificed. Going to the generous-
hearted Frenchman with a pitiful story of woes, Harris
declared that Harrison (the tenor) stood ready to take
the theatre off his hands and pay him a handsome

bonus, provided Fechter could be induced to cancel his engagement. Touched in his weakest point, his heart, Fechter consented to withdraw, and on a Saturday morning wrote Mr. Harris to that effect. On the following Monday night Mr. Charles Kean appeared at the Princess's in "Hamlet"! The story about Harrison had been a ruse. "Hamlet" with Kean will take as well as with Fechter, thought Mr. Harris, but again did he reckon without his public. Finding out the mistake, Mr. Kean conveniently managed to turn his foot on this first night, and did not appear for a fortnight, when "Hamlet" was quietly ignored. Once more did the manager beg Fechter to return, and once more did he refuse.

This scurvy trick was most unfortunate for Fechter, as it prevented him from acting during the Exhibition, — a consummation he had devoutly wished. Weary of managerial chicanery, he became lessee of the Lyceum, which opened on the 10th of January, 1863, with "The Duke's Motto." For seven months this drama drew great houses, until Fechter, satiated with *Henri de Lagardère*, dropped it in the full tide of success. Reopening with "Bel Demonio" on the 15th of October, this highly colored drama bade fair to rival "The Duke's Motto" in popularity, when Fechter's evil genius stepped between him and fortune. On the one hundred and seventy-fifth night Fechter, in making his entrance through a window, caught his spur in the sill, and fell so violently as to drive the hook of his scabbard through his right hand. Ready to faint with pain, he yet went through the scene, and even finished the play, not realizing how dangerous a wound he had received. Arising the next morning with the intention of acting, his physician found him shaving himself.

"You had better go back to bed," said the doctor.

"O no, I shall act to-night."

"Indeed ! we 'll see about that. Do you feel anything queer about the jaws?"

"No."

"Well, keep very quiet. I 'll return in a few hours."

Return he did, and, as he expected, found Fechter in bed, but fortunately with no symptoms of lockjaw. The exhausted actor and manager lay for three weeks in a state of stupor, rarely conscious, saving when food was administered. Escaping the terrible death of lock-jaw, he went to the Isle of Wight, where he gained strength so rapidly as to venture to act "Bel Demonio" for the benefit of the sufferers from the Sheffield inundation. In acknowledging the generous donation of two hundred and three pounds, the entire receipts, the Mayor of Sheffield offered to return eighty pounds, the fund having reached the sum necessary to meet the most desperate cases. "Give the rest to the poor," Fechter replied.

The night following this benefit Fechter broke down, and three more weeks passed before he was able to resume his profession. Such contretemps were not likely to advance the interests of a theatre of which he was the pecuniary attraction ; and the Shakespeare tercentenary celebration being announced for April 23, 1864, Fechter determined to bring out "Hamlet" with every possible effect. His orders were not fulfilled until a fortnight later, and the indignant manager indulged in the luxury of a lawsuit. " Hamlet " then ran forty nights.

The autumn season of 1864 opened with Paul Meurice's comedy-drama of " The King's Butterfly." Splendidly gotten up, and introducing Fechter's favorite blood-mare Minerva, who understood French and English equally well, — knew almost as much as her namesake, and acted in a wonderfully human way, — the new sensation endured three or four months, when it was withdrawn to make way for " The Mountebank," which was no more nor less than " Belphegor " entirely rewritten by Charles Dickens, with a child's part introduced to display the great dramatic ability of Fechter's son Paul, then a child of seven. The counterpart of his father in appearance, — it was like seeing him through the small end of an opera-glass, — the lad astonished everybody by his acting. On the first night he brought tears into the eyes of the old artists around him, and introduced bits of " business " that amazed even his father ; but Paul soon tired of the many repetitions and, being a pet with the ladies, found it much more interesting to play to the boxes, and be showered with bonbons, than to lose himself in his part.[1]

" How can you smile at those women when the situations are so tragic ? " asked the father in despair.

[1] On November 29, 1847, Fechter married M'lle Roebert, a most estimable woman and a pensionnaire of the Comédie Française. The offspring of this marriage were a son Paul and a daughter Marie. The former is studying for the law. The latter is an operatic singer.

"Well, but father, you don't really die, you know. It is n't true. It 's only make-believe. We all come home alive and enjoy ourselves, so where 's the harm?"

Fechter saw that the stage would be Paul's ruin, and, regardless of pecuniary loss, withdrew the drama, bringing out " The Roadside Inn," a new version of " Robert Macaire." This novel rendering of an old friend drew immense houses for three months, and might have continued indefinitely but for the Prince of Wales's desire to witness a performance of " Ruy Blas."

" If I comply with your request, I 'll surely ruin the future of ' The Roadside Inn,' " said Fechter.

" Not if you give ' Ruy Blas ' on a Saturday night and by royal command," argued the Prince.

Very doubtful as to consequences, Fechter complied. The papers waxed furious at the idea of royalty leaving native talent unhonored, and commanding a performance at the theatre of what they were pleased to call " a French importation." The treasury took two hundred and thirty pounds, ten pounds more than the theatre held, and enthusiasm ran riot. But alas for " The Roadside Inn " ! The next Monday's receipts drooped to seventy pounds, and the previously successful drama fell into a rapid decline. The public is a queer monster, far queerer than his Royal Highness the Prince of Wales ever dreamed, and the only sop Fechter could throw to it was " Ruy Blas." Victor Hugo reigned until the close of the summer season of 1865.

Fifteen years ago the Lyceum was not a theatre adapted to the legitimate drama.    When Fechter assumed its management he did so as a *pis aller ;* and, while earnestly longing to produce other Shakespearian plays, he found himself hedged in by fate.    He thought in prose what no less a man than Garrick had written in verse : —

> " If an empty house, the actor's curse,
>   Shows us our *Lears* and *Hamlets* lose their force,
>   Unwilling we must change the nobler scene,
>   And in our turn present you *Harlequin,* —
>   Quit poets and set carpenters to work,
>   Show gaudy scenes, or mount the vaulting Turk ;
>   For though we actors one and all agree
>   Boldly to struggle for our — vanity,
>   If want comes in, misfortune must retreat ;
>   Our first great ruling passion is — to eat ! "

With this idea of eating in view, Fechter began the autumn of 1865 with " The Watch-Cry," a drama in three acts, founded on the story of the three brothers Salviati.    It held up its head quite firmly for two months ; but as Fechter represented a dumb man, and confined his language to that of pantomime, the people declared that he did not talk enough.    " We want to hear as well as see him."    Wishing to gratify this amiable desire Fechter produced " The Master of Ravenswood," on December 23, 1865, and made so deep an impression in the romantic *Edgar* that he played nothing else for the remainder of the season.

September, 1866, saw Fechter personating *Hamlet* for two weeks.    Going from one extreme to the other

he revived " The Corsican Brothers," which attracted
excellent audiences for one month. Then came Fechter's own drama of " Rouge et Noir," founded on
" Thirty Years of a Gambler's Life." It was pronounced
good work, and lived luxuriously for one hundred and
fifty nights.

Feeling himself utterly incompetent to circumvent
the harpies who fattened upon his treasury, Fechter
determined to retire from the lesseeship of the Lyceum,
and henceforth confine himself to his proper sphere of
acting and stage direction. Behind the scenes Fechter
was a master ; before them he was, like most artists, a
child. Wishing to close his theatre with éclat he produced " The Lady of Lyons," and created so great a
furore in *Claude Melnotte* as to astonish even Bulwer.
It ran seventy nights, the curtain falling last upon it.on
November 16, 1867. Then followed the great success
at the Adelphi of " No Thoroughfare," dramatized by
Dickens, Wilkie Collins, and Fechter, and acted one
hundred and fifty-one times. Fechter's powerful rendering of *Obenreizer* made the drama ; and no sooner
was it withdrawn than he went to Paris with Dickens to
superintend the rehearsals of its French adaptation,
" L'Abîme." Returning to the Adelphi, Fechter won
double laurels for one hundred nights in his clever
drama of " Monte Cristo," after which he appeared in
" Black and White," the joint work of himself and Wilkie Collins.

Not having visited the provinces since 1865, when
his circuit had been limited to Glasgow, Birmingham,
and Liverpool, Fechter gave eight months of 1869 to a

tour through Great Britain and Ireland. Even Liverpool acknowledged his power. This city is not greatly given to legitimate drama; nevertheless Liverpool wanted to see Fechter in "Hamlet." "Very well," said Fechter, "'Black and White' cannot be withdrawn, because it is filling the theatre; but if you like I will give you one act of 'Hamlet' every night until finished, and you shall have it after the drama."

The Liverpudlians readily assented to this arrangement, and, putting all his intensity into each act, Fechter never acted *Hamlet* as equally as on those five nights. Liverpool was an easy conquest, but not so Manchester. This good town had a grievance. Years before, Manchester had commanded, had petitioned, had finally implored Fechter to come to them, but it was not until this season that he was able to respond to the prayer. Then Manchester arose in all her might to resent a prolonged absence, which she chose to consider a slight. The world may think what it pleases of London as the heart and head of Great Britain, but Manchester has opinions of its own, pre-eminent among which is the religious conviction that Manchester is the centre of the solar system. Consequently, when Fechter did appear at the Theatre Royal, it became incumbent upon a club clique to punish him for his previous indifference. So the clique decided that Fechter should play to empty benches until the production of "Hamlet," when the entire solar system should shine upon the star. Feeling the injustice of such treatment, and determined to preserve his personal as well as professional dignity, Fechter held the cards in his own hands and won the game. Playing to audiences of three and four hundred, he never acted better in his life. For those who did come to see him he felt that he owed all that he could give ; for those who childishly attempted to humiliate him he inserted a card at the head of the play-bills, in which Mr. Fechter took great pleasure in announcing that his engagement would not be prolonged after the performances of " Ruy Blas " and " Black and White " ! He was as good as his word, and the clubs of Manchester discovered that for once they had found their match.

Accepting an offer to visit the United States, Fechter hurried back to London, and, after fourteen farewell performances at the Princess's of " Ruy Blas," " Lady of Lyons," and " Hamlet," set sail for America. " Come back soon," said the Prince of Wales on that last of farewell nights. " Remember that we cannot get on without you." Well might royalty confess as much, for it will be long ere England salutes the peer of that " French importation," Charles Albert Fechter.

# FECHTER IN THE UNITED STATES.

## 1870–1879.

———◆———

*" My fame is a mere ephemeron, at the command of caprice. The same breath that nourishes the flame to-day, puts it out to-morrow."*

EDMUND KEAN.

# FECHTER IN THE UNITED STATES.

—◆—

TWELVE years have passed since Charles Albert Fechter, unheralded save by a few words˅of praise from the pen of that best of dramatic critics, Charles Dickens, made his début in New York. He came, he was heard, he conquered. An eager public assembled in Niblo's Garden on the 10th of January, 1870, to witness "Ruy Blas." The effect produced was identical with that produced in London and recorded in the *Times*, on Fechter's first appearance as an English actor : —

"As to the manner in which M. Fechter would speak English the mind of the audience was soon at ease, and there is that music in his voice which would sound equally well through the medium of any language. *Ruy's* narrative of his sufferings and his love, and the small delicate touches by which he indicated his uneasiness under a master's control, carried him well through the first act, and though the great scenes of the piece were yet to come, it was easy to foresee that the manner of their execution would be in every way satisfactory. The second act was an immense advance on the first. Nothing could be finer of its kind than *Ruy's* declaration of love to the *Queen*, so exquisitely

was the fire of passion tempered by the feeling of respectful devotion, and with such eloquence of words
and action was the text poured forth.    There are
not many actors who succeed even in ordinary love-
scenes ; and few indeed could effect an exhibition of
that idolatrous form of passion which inspired so many
poets of the chivalric ages.    The misery to which the
virtuous impostor is exposed when his master suddenly
reappears and compels him to do petty menial offices
while he is still in the plenitude of his power, — the
terribly jarring conflict between the aspiring mind of
the statesman and the bounden condition of the lackey,
— was represented with wondrous force and abun-
dance of detail.    But it was in the last act that the
triumph of the actor reached its culminating point, —
the act in which the valet appears as the defender of the
*Queen* against the machinations of his villainous master.
The concentration of passionate rage with which he ac-
costed his oppressor, the obvious feeling that he was
throwing from his soul a burden that had long crushed
it to the dust, elicited that continued succession of
plaudits which is only heard when an audience is excited in the highest degree.    From the moment when
*Ruy* snatches the sword from his master's side (an action which of itself produced an electrical effect) to
the fall of the curtain, when the valet dies happy in the
conviction that he is loved not under false colors, but
with the livery actually present to the mind's eye of his
royal mistress, M. Fechter had the audience completely
in his grasp and could do with them as he pleased.
The shouts which invited him to the front of the curtain

were the certain indications of an unequivocal and brilliant success."

To me this Anglo-Franco-Piemontese-Teuton was a revelation. I had been, from childhood, under the influence of the natural school of acting. The exquisite comedy of the Théâtre Français, the grandeur and force of Ristori and. Salvini, the incomparable humor of Charles Dickens the reader, had been a liberal education in dramatic art. I wondered if I should ever see upon the stage such a lover as Garrick and Barry are said to have been. It seemed to me twelve years ago, and it seems to me in the present year of our Lord, that he is the finest actor who best depicts the noblest of all passions. " O Art, my art, thou art much ! " exclaims Aurora Leigh, "but love is more ! Art symbolizes heaven ; but God is Love and means Heaven." If love be the divine passion, the delineation of love should be the actor's highest aspiration. To attain his ideal should be the actor's crowning glory. When Charles Fechter as *Ruy Blas* uttered those five small words, " I madly love the queen ; " when he dared to exclaim before *Don Cæsar*, " I love her, that 's all ! " when, dying, he gazed upon his sovereign for the last time, throwing into his face an expression absolutely marvellous in beauty and pathos, I felt that the delineation of love could no further go.

Fechter's appearance in " The Duke's Motto," on January 26, confirmed the public in their enthusiastic admiration. The dual parts of *Henri de Lagardère* and *Æsop the Hunchback* were so thrillingly portrayed as to make the illusion complete. The actor lived in his assumptions, and proved the justice of John Weiss's criticism : —

"When I saw that great genius, Fechter, before he had spoken a word I felt he was the man he was to stand for, and from that time every word and movement was but added proof to my feeling. I had to tear myself away from the man he stood for when I would think of the man he was; and I doubt not, if I could have seen the working of his nature within, I should have found that he was not himself in that hour, but the embodiment of the poet's conception."

Successful in the romantic drama, Fechter, on the 14th of February, played *Hamlet*, a character about which every critic, every confirmed play-goer, and every Shakespearian reader has a preconceived opinion. That he produced a sensation is unquestioned; that his conception was severely criticised is equally true. It was not until he appeared at the Boston Theatre, on February 21, that Fechter received such recognition in "Hamlet" as England had given him. Boston took the new actor to its inmost heart. The enthusiasm excited by his interpretation of Shakespeare increased with representations of "Ruy Blas" and "The Lady of Lyons," and the farewell matinée of Bulwer's play was such an ovation as I have never seen equalled in any country. Gray-headed men shouted with delight at the close of the fourth act. Not content with the frantic waving of handkerchiefs, women took off their hats and bonnets, and performed strange gymnastics with them. Again and again were Fechter and his excellent assistant, Miss Carlotta Leclercq, called before the curtain, and applause only ended when physical exhaustion set in.

People were Fechter mad. No dinner was complete without him. The man fascinated as .much as the actor. He possessed the animal magnetism with which great actors and orators are generally endowed.

After visiting Philadelphia professionally, Fechter returned to the Boston Theatre and, on the 20th of March, opened in "The Duke's Motto " with all his previous success. "No Thoroughfare " followed.

> "Who wrote 'No Thoroughfare '?
> Surely not Boz.
> Collins it was, —
> He wrote 'No Thoroughfare.'"

During his visit to this country, Dickens took up a copy of the last of the "Christmas Stories," and marked with a pencil such portions as were his own. The book thus marked, which would be highly valued now, was by some ill luck mislaid, but the clever man of letters, to whom it belonged, declares the proportion of Dickens to Collins to have been exceedingly small. "No Thoroughfare " will never be known to posterity as other than a child of Wilkie Collins's brain, as like its father as a child can be that has been fed on Dickens. To say what portions of "No Thoroughfare " Dickens actually wrote would be presumptuous ; but it is probable that after talking over the plot together, — a plot that is pre-eminently Collinsish, — Dickens started the story, conceived the character of *Joey Ladle*, and, with a touch here and there, left the rest to his collaborateur. "Gentlemen, it is all wery well for you, that has been accustomed to take your wine into your systems by the conwivial channel of your throttles, to put a lively face upon it ; but I have been accustomed to take *my* wine in at the pores of the skin, and, took that way, it acts different. It acts depressing. It's one thing to charge your glasses in a dining-room with a Hip Hurrah and Jolly Companions Every One, and it's another thing to be charged yourself, through the pores, in a low, dark cellar and a mouldy atmosphere. It makes all the difference betwixt bubbles and wapors. I've been a cellarman my life through, with my mind fully given to the business. What's the consequence? I'm as muddled a man as lives — you won't find a muddleder man than me — nor yet you won't find my equal in molloncholly. Sing of Filling the bumper fair, Every drop you sprinkle O'er the brow of care Smooths away a wrinkle? Yes. P'r'aps so. But try filling yourself through the pores, under ground, when you don't want it." If Dickens did not originate *Joey Ladle* and his quaint conceit, Dickens never originated anything. Successful as a story, " No Thoroughfare " was no less successful when, dramatized in 1867, it was brought out by Fechter at the Adelphi, in London, and acted one hundred and fifty-one times. It was only withdrawn in England to be produced in Paris under the name of " L'Abîme," the French adaptation being Fechter's, and the rehearsals being superintended by Dickens and himself.

With such prestige, the announcement of the production of this drama furnished tea-tables with no small amount of gossip. Boston's first and last families and Boston's brains were at this *premièze*. All the cultivated clever women, whose society makes this city so exceptional, were there. There sat Longfellow, looking like an intellectual "King Lear," editors whose hands were oftenest the first to start applause, James T. Fields, and many another. And the drama itself? It is clever. Though the first performance dragged its slow length along to the witching hour of twelve, few left the theatre. This is the greatest compliment Boston can offer an artist, as the suburban population, tied to inflexible trains and horse-cars, generally get up and walk out in agonizing ignorance of dénouements. There are those who have never seen the last act of anything, and await a future existence before they shall be able to finish their uncompleted lives. Apart from the prologue, which can never be interesting, as no interesting characters appear in it, and apart from bits of scenes for subordinate characters that must always bore more or less, for the reason that little parts are rarely well played — "No Thoroughfare" commands constant attention. Of course, it is sensational. Wilkie Collins never wrote anything that was not highly so, and the drama is a condensation rather than a dilution of the story, altered by Fechter in several important respects to meet the requirements of the stage.

In delineating *Obenreizer*, a passionate villain, Fechter gave one more proof of his great versatility. His easy colloquial acting in the beginning was delightful, and in the fourth tableau he was masterly. His quick transitions from repose to action, at one moment giving advice, at another stealthily endeavoring to gain possession of the receipt; his equally stealthy attempt to overcome *Vendale*, thwarted by the entrance of *Joey Ladle*; his relapse into the old familiar manner, and final urging of *Vendale* to go himself to Switzerland and bear him (*Obenreizer*) company, who, strangely enough, is forced to make the same journey; his inviting *Vendale* to dine, that they may start together and he see *Marguerite*, — were phases as marvellous in combination as the changes of the kaleidoscope.

When, in the fifth tableau, *Obenreizer* returns after the drug has taken effect, his cat-like approach to the bed in search of the forged receipt; his terror upon discovering that *Vendale* sleeps in the chair by the fire; *Vendale's* momentary return to consciousness, and the story upon *Obenreizer's* lips that he has had a bad dream about his friend that caused his return; *Vendale's* invitation to remain; *Obenreizer's* inclination to kill *Vendale* while asleep; his feeling for the receipt in *Vendale's* pocket, and the unexpected appearance of a guide rapping out four o'clock, the hour of starting over the Alps, just as he is about to seize the receipt, were all so thrilling in pantomime as to make the spectator watch the scene with bated breath, believing it to be real.

The seventh and last tableau showed Fechter at his best in the exquisite pathos of action and expression, as *Obenreizer*, dying of despair and nervous exhaustion, looked upon the woman he loved.

" No Thoroughfare " was succeeded by " Don Cæsar de Bazan " and " Ruy Blas." The universal favorite
bade farewell for the season on April 16, when he
acted in French for the benefit of the French Comedy
Company that sorely needed financial help. No one
was readier than he to give his services to a worthy
cause.

Again in New York, Fechter played an engagement
at the French Theatre (now Haverly's Fourteenth
Street Theatre) which lasted from April 27 to May
23, during which time " The Lady of Lyons," " Don
Cæsar de Bazan," " Ruy Blas," " Hamlet" and " The
Corsican Brothers " were produced. In New York
Fechter was admired, in Boston he founded a religion.
Small blame to him then for preferring the Modern
Athens. He dreamed of what might be done for
dramatic art in the town which he said should hereafter be his home. He found a loving friend and dis-
ciple in Arthur Cheney, proprietor of a new theatre,
the management of which Fechter accepted with enthusiasm. He would give up starring ; no one better
appreciated the evils of a system which abolishes stock
companies. He, Fechter, would prove theories by
example, and the land of his adoption should have a
school of acting the influence of which would be universal. It was delightful to hear Fechter talk on dramatic art, of which he was master, and it was no less
delightful to witness Arthur Cheney's eagerness to carry
out Fechter's plans. All Boston was alive with excitement. A new dramatic era was about to dawn.

First came the naming of the theatre. The amount

of brains required in this matter is only known to such as have attempted to christen a book, a play, a boat, or a patent.

" Master Field, the player," writes Taylor the water-poet, "riding up Fleet Street at a great pace, a gentleman called him, and asked him what play was played that day. He being angry to be staied on so frivolous a demand, answered that he might see what play was plaied *upon every poste*. ' I cry you mercy,' said the gentleman, ' I tooke you for a *poste*, you rode so fast.' " This Master Field, otherwise Nat Field, one of the earliest dramatists, little dreamed that two hundred and seventy years after Shakespeare, himself, and comrades had strutted their brief hours upon the stage of that Globe which may be called the mother of English theatres, a new world would seek, by the resurrection of a name, to link itself with an illustrious past. Yet this came about in the baptism of Fechter's theatre, the curtain of which rose September 12, 1870, upon the plot and passion of " Monte Cristo." It was a glad night for Boston. Our fathers had grown garrulous over the palmy days of the drama. What would they say to a stock company including Fechter, James W. Wallack, C. H. Vandenhoff, G. H. Griffiths, W. J. Lemoyne, the brothers Leclercq, H. F. Daly, Miss Carlotta Leclercq, Mrs. Chanfrau, Mrs. Melinda Jones, Miss Mary Cary, and a score of lesser though most useful lights? A king among pygmies is a sorry sight. To be king among princes is the only ambition worthy of genius. The Drama was to be cared for irrespective of individual actors. The system of starring was to be abolished. The motto of the Globe was to be "Equality and Fraternity." There was to be a constant succession of new works, in which the honors of performance were to be equally divided, and Victorien Sardou was to be asked to write specially for the new theatre.

Boston thought the millennium in art had come. Alas, Boston reckoned without its master of revels. I wish it were not necessary to show other than the bright side of Fechter's career, but the truth must be told. Boston's dreams, Arthur Cheney's dreams, of a model theatre, were to vanish into thin air. There were dissensions, misunderstandings, from the beginning, all of which might have been avoided had Fechter been a reasonable man of business instead of an undisciplined genius. There was a twist in Fechter's mind that no human being could make straight by argument or any other means. Personally I never held him responsible for either words or deeds. His blood was too hot for reason. His father possessed an ungovernable temper, aggravated by drink, which he bequeathed to his brilliant son. No one was ever less fitted to command, for the reason that he had never learned to command himself.

Poor Arthur Cheney's life was not a bed of roses. Devoted to Fechter, anxious for the success of his own theatre, he saw with dismay a storm arise between Fechter and Wallack, the story of which is told by the combatants in the following correspondence relating to the part of *Don Salluste*, for which Wallack had been cast by his manager, Fechter : —

" My Dear Fechter, — I have received the play, and do not like the part of *Don Salluste* at all. I would rather not play it.

> Yours truly,
> J. W. Wallack."

" My Dear Wallack, — I sent you the part of *Don Salluste* to study, not to judge. I should as soon think of asking your permission to cast you as *Joseph Surface* as *Don Salluste.* I beg of you to reconsider your note and accept the part, or your services will be useless here, and your engagement at an end this very week. I consider *Don Salluste* the best part in the play, and would much rather act it than *Ruy Blas.* If you say so we will alternate the part . . . . And I am, my dear Wallack,

> Yours truly,
> Charles Fechter."

" Sir, — I consider that no other prefix is necessary after your letter of this date . . . . I shall have no further correspondence with you in relation to my engagement at the Globe, as I in no way recognize your right to interfere. Mr. Cheney is the sole party to whom I am engaged and to whom I shall look for fulfilment of the business contract made. Had you adhered to the agreement as understood by us, or had you intended to keep your word as given in the presence of Mr. Cheney, this need not have occurred. As it is, I decline further correspondence of any nature with you.    Yours,

> J. W. Wallack."

Surely so serious a tempest never arose in so small a teapot. But, with all Fechter's irritability of temper, he certainly had the right of it in casting Wallack for *Don Salluste;* and why that usually sensible actor refused the part is beyond present comprehension.

Like a shuttlecock Arthur Cheney was tossed from one battledoor to the other, reporters from all over the country interviewed both actors, and great was the scandal thereof.

" The difficulty with Fechter," said Wallack to a journalist, " is that he does n't understand men, and especially me. He 's too high and mighty. All he had to do was to slap me on the back and say ' Here Jim, let's take a drink ; I dare say we are both wrong,' and I would have given in at once. Instead of that, he gets his back up, won't play at all, and puts the management in a hole." When this same journalist called on Fechter, the actor-manager said, " Nobody can manage Wallack but myself. I can't manage him in this matter at all. All he had to do was to ask me to take a glass of wine and arrange it amicably, but he is so stubborn. He 's like a mule, my dear boy ; and so I wait till he is ready to make the advance, for after all I am in the right." It is said that in less than an hour the two actors met at the house of this common friend, and both laughed heartily when their host narrated his experience with each of them. Actors have been called children of a larger growth. Were there ever greater proofs thereof than are found in this episode? At last there came the climax ; and on December 14, 1870, Fechter, in an injudicious letter addressed

to the editor of the *Boston Traveller*, unveiled the secrets
of the coulisses.   He therein declared his intention
of resigning the management of the Globe Theatre,
" notwithstanding the prayers of and his sincere affection for his friend Cheney."   The story Fechter then
told need not be repeated.   Quarrels die as well as
people.   The truth lay in the fact that Fechter was the
right man in the wrong place.   It is no more than just,
however, to Fechter to reaffirm his statement that " in
assuming management, at a great pecuniary loss, he
had no other views than the benefit of art, the wholesome amusement of the public, and the pride and
comfort of his hearty friend Cheney."   Fechter was
always indifferent to money ; he spent it as fast as he
made it.   He held Boston in high esteem, — and well
he might, as there he found his best friends and warmest
appreciators.   He truly longed to advance dramatic
art.   He did not know himself.

Boston's millennium was brief.   After holding the
stage for twelve weeks, " Monte Cristo " made way for
" Hamlet," " Lady of Lyons," " Ruy Blas " and " Don
Cæsar de Bazan ; " and on December 26 Fechter produced for the first time in this country the drama of
" Black and White," written by Wilkie Collins and
himself.   The public were greatly impressed by Fechter's acting, and liked the drama ; but on January 14,
1871, Fechter trod the stage of the Globe Theatre for
the last time.   The occasion was made a testimonial
benefit to himself, at which he appeared as *Ruy Blas*, —
Miss Carlotta Leclercq playing "A Sheep In Wolf's
Clothing " as an afterpiece.

From this point Fechter's downfall begins. The unhappy temper that wrecked the fortunes of the Globe Theatre lost none of its malign influence on being transplanted to New York. Fechter believed that his dream of a theatre might be realized in the metropolis. The capitalist was found ; the French Theatre was selected. Certainly Fechter showed his fine knowledge of theatrical requirements, both before and behind the footlights, in the changes which were made under his direction ; but the day of misunderstandings set in, and the Lyceum, named after Fechter's London theatre, never knew its creator as manager.

Returning to Europe for a few months in 1872, Fechter reappeared at the Adelphi, London, in March ; when, according to the *Times,* " he was heartily greeted by a numerous and expectant audience, who burst into one unanimous shout of welcome as soon as he became visible on the stage." The drama was " Ruy Blas," in which Fechter exercised all his old charm, — the *Times* declaring that " devotional love, which is the life and soul of so many poems and romances, is expressed by Mr. Fechter with an intensity which is peculiarly his own."

Fechter's next appearance in New York was on April 28, 1873, as *Monte Cristo,* at the Grand Opera House. This drama was followed on June 1 by " The Corsican Brothers," and on June 9 by " Ruy Blas," which was played a week. On December 11 of the same year, Fechter began an engagement at what was to have been his own theatre, the Lyceum. The doors suddenly closed after nine nights of " The Lady of

Lyons." It was pathetic to watch the decadence in popularity of a great actor, a decadence due to the faults of the man.

Four months later, on April 13, 1874, Fechter opened the Park Theater on Broadway, near Twenty-second Street, under William Stuart's management. The attraction was " Love's Penance," a play in three acts, and a prologue adapted by himself from " Le Médecin des Enfants." The first night's audience knew what acting meant, and gave to Fechter the enthusiastic approbation he deserved.

After? The sequel is told by William Winter, in the *Tribune:* " The play was too long and too sombre, but Fechter never acted better ; and in a more artistic community the actor would have saved the piece, and put money in the manager's purse. But New York was not Paris. Personally Fechter had ceased to be popular, through no one's fault but his own, I grieve to admit ; and after twenty-three performances, ' Love's Penance ' was withdrawn." Here is the story, in five words : *New York was not Paris.* Paris, as a rule, recognizes art, irrespective of individuals ; New York looks at art through personality. Fechter ignored or quarrelled with those upon whom his success depended. It was pitiful.

*Karl* in " Love's Penance " was Fechter's last creation. From this time forward he was content with the repertoire that had made him famous. In some towns, especially Boston, he exercised all his old power ; in others, he was not appreciated. In 1876 Fechter fell upon the ice, and broke his leg. This misfortune made him physically infirm, and cast additional gloom upon his career. The end was not long in coming. Appearing in public by flashes, Fechter sought seclusion on his farm, which he bought in July, 1873, having always declared that the farmer was the happiest and most independent of men. To begin a career in Paris, and to end it in the little village of Rockland Centre, Bucks County, three miles from Quakertown, and two hours from Philadelphia by the North Pennsylvania Railroad, is as strange a contrast as can well befall mortal. In an old unpretentious country-house, a few feet from the highway, the ideal stage-lover passed the greater part of the last three years of his life. The farm consisted of fifty-seven acres. Fechter's summer sitting-room was hung with fire-arms; for he delighted in field-sports, and was as fine a shot as he was a fencer. Dickens did not love dogs more dearly. Five of these noble brutes shared the actor's room and table. They were his companions in all his excursions, saving when he wielded the fishing-rod, with which he was very skilful.

Nature could not restore Fechter to health. For years — ever after the attack of typhoid fever in Paris — his digestive organs were greatly impaired; and it was not unusual for his stomach to be distended with gas like a drum, causing great suffering, and rendering clothing insupportable. Yet in this condition he enchanted many an audience! Imagination triumphs over matter. But matter has its revenge in the end. Fechter disappointed the public again and again, — the public taking their revenge by attributing his non-appearance to dissipation. He was on the road to the grave. The spring of 1879 found him in precarious health, and bad became worse as summer appoached. The malady being of the liver and digestive organs, Fechter's agony was intense. At last Fechter was confined to the house, and, gradually sinking into a stupor, died at six o'clock on the morning of Aug. 5, 1879.

Had Fechter been as complete a man as he was an actor, his death would have been a calamity. Accepting facts, his best friends realized that he passed away none too soon for his reputation. Months previous, he had in his own mind bade farewell to the stage. When, on his last visit to New York, he consulted physicians concerning his disease, Fechter exclaimed mournfully, after witnessing a dramatic performance : " Poor —— ! he little knows how his fat stomach affects his cavaliership ; but in his ludicrousness, I read my own fate. I am done with the stage forever." Friends laughed ; whereupon he grew eloquent on the necessity of physical fitness to artistic success. Love was opposed to obesity, and he would renounce *Ruy Blas* before *Ruy Blas* renounced him. Is it not pathetic that an actor's brains should not weigh in the balance against an actor's paunch? *Romeo* may be divine, yet if *Romeo* be fat, the world wants him not.

He who lives in the glare of the footlights is doomed to have his failings proclaimed from the housetops. Human nature is prone to believe the worst, and attributed Fechter's death to drink. On being told that report gave credence to such a belief, Fechter's physician replied, after a post-mortem examination : " There is nothing to indicate such a condition. I do not believe that he has been a drinking man of late. We had great difficulty in getting him to swallow stimulants to keep up his strength. He refused at first. He was conscious until nearly the last, and suffered very much. I don't believe his illness was brought on by the use of liquor."

Followed by one or two intimate friends and a few acquaintances, Charles Fechter's remains were on August 8 placed in the receiving vault of Mt. Vernon Cemetery, Philadelphia. On the 20th of June, 1880, they were laid in the grave. Fechter's monument, representing a bust of the actor with bay leaves and laurel carved around it, bears the inscription, " Genius has taken its flight to God." In taking that flight, the soul has found the light that genius failed to give.

Those of us who believe in Fechter's greatness do not care to remember the blots on the escutcheon. He was a benefactor in dramatic art. Let that fact suffice. Personally he could be delightful, and I owe to him hours upon hours of instruction as well as of entertainment. He believed in the stage, and no one was ever more lucid or fluent in its exposition. He was not one to brook contradiction, however, and I should have sooner thought of playing *Hamlet* than of opposing his pet opinions. Like Landor he possessed "a proud complacency and scornful strength," a resentful impatience ; like Landor he was choleric. Like Landor he had that to impart which was worth learning. In Dickens's household the master was called " Mr. Always Right," while his friend Fechter received the sobriquet of " Mr. Never Wrong." Here was the rock which wrecked a noble career. *Faiblesse vaut vice* was his life-long motto ; it was his inherited curse. If nature has endowed us with less waywardness and more self-control than fell to the lot of Charles Fechter, the more reason have we to thank God and to encircle with charity the memory of an unhappy genius.

" Rest, perturbed spirit."

# FECHTER'S "HAMLET."

# FECHTER'S "HAMLET."

Of all Fechter's repertoire given in this country, *Hamlet* was the only character that fully called out his resources; and, whether or not his conception be acknowledged as Shakespeare's, he strangely moved his audiences. Who, however, is presumptuous enough to proclaim Shakespeare's conception of "Hamlet"? From Voltaire, who declared "Hamlet" to be the work of a drunken savage, to Goethe, who would have made innumerable changes in the plot, — from Coleridge to our own brilliant Lowell, — "there has been much throwing about of brains." That Shakespeare has not "revisited the glimpses of the moon" to tell us what he does mean, is strong evidence against the theory of modern Spiritualism. Never have written words, the Bible excepted, inspired a like amount of controversy; and as Catholic and Protestant, Episcopalian and Radical, Presbyterian and Unitarian, find their creeds in the Testaments, so do critics find authority for their various dogmas concerning "Hamlet." While no two entirely sympathize, shall the right of private judgment be abolished? and because a great actor disagrees with certain great writers, shall he be crucified and told that his is not *Shakespeare's Hamlet?* It is an easy criticism to make, — Shakespeare being "safely stowed," and no contradiction possible.　It is so cheap as to fall first from the lips of those who have never given "Hamlet" a thought, and are, therefore, quite prepared to pass judgment.

"It is n't Shakespeare's *Hamlet*," exclaimed an illiterate man who sat behind me at the theatre one night.　"It is n't right, you know.　He does n't give you the proper accents.　It 's a foreigner's interpretation."

"Well, but — *Hamlet*'s a foreigner, is n't he?" asked a timid little woman, in a timid little voice.

"Yes," responded the critic, with a somewhat puzzled expression of face, "he 's a foreigner, he 's a foreigner, but," and then exultation broke through the trouble, — "but *you see it 's an English play!*"

Argument ceased.　Everybody was carried away by the illiterate man's superior intelligence.　Nevertheless, the timid little woman *did* murmur that it was very interesting and there must be something in it, as heretofore she had always gone to sleep over "Hamlet."

If people would only cast commentators aside and read "Hamlet" by the light of their own understanding, they would be surprised to find how much clearer the text is than writers are willing to have it appear.[1]

---

[1] One is tempted to "wrangle gently" with Mr. White for his statement that the *Ghost* does not appear in the third act, *Hamlet* being the victim of an optical delusion.　Does not the *Ghost* speak to *Hamlet?*　Why is not the *Ghost* as real in the third as in the first act?　Merely because invisible to the

Fechter's *Hamlet* was not the introspective student of tradition. He was a man of the world, in the noblest sense of the term, of joyous disposition, whose temper — and here he agreed with Goethe — assumed its mournful tinge upon the death of his father and the unseemly marriage of his mother. "Not reflective or sorrowful by nature, reflection and sorrow had become for him a heavy obligation." The *Queen* refers to him as " my too much changed son," and the *King* marvels at *Hamlet's* transformation : —

*Queen*, and visible to *Horatio* and *Marcellus?* This is nothing new in supernatural scenes. " Be subject to no sight but thine and mine," says *Prospero* to *Ariel*, " invisible to every eyeball else ; " and *Ariel* curvets unseen of mortals. *Hamlet* would have doubted his senses had not the *Guards* and the cooler-headed *Horatio* beheld the *Ghost ;* but how contrary to the dead *King's* tender nature to make himself visible to the *Queen*, who, already plunged in agony, would probably be crazed by so awful a spectacle as the apparition of her murdered husband ?

And with regard to Wittenberg, which seems to be the source of so much discussion, there is nothing to indicate *Hamlet's* still being a student. Overcome with grief, disgusted with the world, he talks of going to his old university town where he passed his youth, and where he is most likely to meet true friends, among them *Horatio.* He is easily dissuaded by his mother, and Wittenberg is brought to him in the guise of fellow-students. From first to last the text infers *Hamlet's* long acquaintance with the court and outside world. His welcome to his old friend, " Horatio, or I do forget myself," denotes that the two have not met for some time. *Rosencrantz* and *Guildenstern* are spoken of as

" Being of so young days brought up with him ; "

and *Hamlet* conjures them " by the consonancy of our youth."

> " So I call it,
> Since nor th' exterior nor the inward man
> Resembles that it was."

" I have of late lost all my mirth, foregone all custom of exercises," *Hamlet* states; by which we get a glimpse of a boon companion, " the observed of all observers," one " loved of the distracted multitude," — who delights in all manner of sports, who up to the last moment is so sensitive of his prowess in fencing as to be somewhat jealous of *Laertes's* reputation, and long to cross weapons with him.

His first impulse in grief is to commit suicide, — ever the panacea of hot-blooded sanguine temperaments. No civilized country can rival France in the number of its suicides, yet no people are possessed of equal *esprit* and buoyancy. But *Hamlet* is a good Catholic. The Everlasting has " fixed his canon 'gainst self-slaughter ; " and, though he twice meditates taking his life, he is restrained by religious faith. He is brave and daring, as a soldier ought to be. He is not afraid of his father's *Ghost*, for, on hearing of its appearance, he quickly exclaims, " I would I had been there," and " I will speak to it though hell itself should gape, and bid me hold my peace." Hence he is awed, not terrified, by the *Ghost's* presence. The *Ghost* makes night hideous, because it shakes his disposition " with thoughts beyond the reaches of our souls." Is this the language of a man given to cloistered musings and inward living? How can *Hamlet* possess

> " Courtier's, soldier's, scholar's eye, tongue, sword,"

and lead the life of a seer? It is impossible. He is first courtier and lastly scholar, be it observęd. He is a lover of acting, he is an acute critic, and therefore must be *of* the world, as well as *in* it. Introverted minds take little pleasure in the studies to which *Hamlet* evidently gave much time. *Hamlet's* humor is so deeply implanted that even in the most solemn moments he cannot refrain from apposite punning. It is carried even to grimness over " this fellow in the cellarage." This extreme from grave to gay is not an attribute of introversion, but quite accords with the nature of such a man as Fechter put before us.

Fechter left no doubt as to *Hamlet's* passionate love for *Ophelia,* and truly it was grateful to see the meaning of the text fulfilled. A man who " hath given countenance to his speech with almost all the holy vows of heaven," who begs " dear Ophelia " to

> " Doubt that the stars are fire;
> Doubt that the sun doth move;
> Doubt truth to be a liar;
> But never doubt I love; "

who over her grave declares " that forty thousand brothers could not, with all their quantity of love, make up his sum," and who immediately upon the assumption of madness falls to such perusal of *Ophelia's* face " as he would draw it," and

> " Raised a sigh so piteous and profound,
> As it did seem to shatter all his bulk
> And end his being,"

must be a much more intense lover than actors and Shakespearian commentators have heretofore admitted.

If words mean anything, they mean that *Hamlet's* passion is far stronger than *Ophelia's*. With his intellect and unusual depth of feeling it must of necessity be so ; and if *Ophelia* goes mad, it is because she has less character to withstand sorrow.

Never was Fechter's *Hamlet* at any time really mad, Coleridge and the Kembles (Charles Kemble excepted) to the contrary notwithstanding. He carried out what Lowell has since admirably written : " If Shakespeare himself, without going mad, could so observe and remember all the abnormal symptoms as to be able to reproduce them in *Hamlet*, why should it be beyond the power of *Hamlet* to reproduce them in himself? If you deprive *Hamlet* of reason, there is no truly tragic motive left. He would be a fit subject for bedlam, but not for the stage. We might have pathology enough, but no pathos. Ajax first becomes tragic when he recovers his wits. If *Hamlet* is irresponsible, the whole play is a chaos. That he is not so might be proved by evidence enough, were it not labor thrown away."

True to his times, *Hamlet* does not scruple to take life when it comes between him and the work of his destiny. " By Heaven, I 'll make a ghost of him that lets me," is the threat launched at even so dear a friend as *Horatio*. " I find thee apt " in revenge, says the *Ghost ;* and quicker than thought *Hamlet* dedicates his life to one fell purpose, beginning by wiping away all " trivial fond records," — *Ophelia's* love. Nevertheless he is held back by " a wise skepticism," " the first attribute of a good critic," which suggests the possibility of the spirit's being a devil. Fechter's *Hamlet*

was restrained by reasonable doubt, not vacillation of
purpose, and no sooner caught " " the conscience of
the King " than he could drink hot blood. He did
not kill the *King* at prayers, because of that Catholic
faith which would send this same villain to heaven, and
thus kill all revenge, which is the motive of his action.

> " Would I had met my dearest *foe in heaven,*
> Or ever I had seen that day," —

his mother's second wedding day, — is the heaviest
curse that *Hamlet* can invoke upon his own head.
Would he then be likely voluntarily to bring about its
fulfilment? He keeps himself in training by self-re-
proach of cowardice, of which there is not the slightest
evidence in deeds. ·He cannot, as he has promised
the *Ghost*,

> " With wings as swift
> As meditation, or the thoughts of love,
> . . *sweep* to . . . revenge,"

and he falls " a-cursing like a very drab," unpacking
his " heart with words," as such natures are very apt to
do when circumstances stay their actions. Without a
moment's hesitation he stabs *Polonius*, but repents the
deed, and is engaged in drawing aside the body when
he is seized and brought *guarded* before the *King*, in
which condition he is unarmed. Hurried with " fiery
quickness " on board a bark for England, there is no
opportunity for action ; but, thoughts being bloody, he
forges letters whereby *Guildenstern* and *Rosencrantz*
— " they are not near my conscience," pleads *Hamlet* — are doomed to death the moment they reach

their destination. Chased by pirates, *Hamlet* alone becomes their prisoner, and returns to Denmark. *Horatio* goes to meet him ; and as they tarry in a graveyard, the burial of *Ophelia* drives him to momentary frenzy. Without weapons, he cannot then and there kill the *King*, nor is the most desperate mind controlled by more than one great passion at a time. In the next scene, which must be immediate, — as not till then does *Hamlet* refer to his escape and plot against his treacherous fellow-students, — he does not hesitate to tell *Horatio* of his purpose to " quit the King with his arm " during the short interval that must elapse ere the fate of *Guildenstern* and *Rosencrantz* is known in Denmark. Being sorry for having forgotten himself to *Laertes*, whom he loves and whom he has wronged, he accepts the challenge of a bout at fencing, that he may then and there apologize to the brother of his adoption, and also gain easy approach to his intended victim, the *King*. He cannot kill the *King* with bated rapier ; but the moment he learns that the weapon in his hand is unbated and envenomed, *Hamlet* stabs the evil genius of the play. The *King* has no doubt of *Hamlet's* capability of murder, as proved by his saying after hearing of the death of *Polonius*, " It had been so with us, had we been there," and by his haste in sending him to England.

Such, from his acting, was Fechter's conception of *Hamlet*, sympathetic to me in all things, except perhaps in this matter of vacillation ; and even here one may make out a strong case. The only lines that can be quoted against Fechter's theory are the few appertaining to the *Ghost's* reappearance.

> "Do you not come your tardy son to chide,
>    That, lapsed in time and passion, lets go by
>    Th' important acting of your dread command?
>    O, say!"

inquires *Hamlet.*

> "*Ghost.* Do not forget. This visitation
>    Is but to whet thy almost blunted purpose."

*Hamlet* but repeats the self-accusation prompted by over-sensibility as to the performance of an awful duty.

"Ah, but what blunted purpose does the *Ghost* come to whet?" asks the reader. Suppose this visitation be to whet *Hamlet's* almost blunted purpose of speaking daggers, but using none? The *Ghost* unlike his former self, says not one word about *Claudius.* He straightway exhorts Hamlet to step between *his mother* and her fighting soul! Whereupon *Hamlet's* tone changes from violent denunciation to soft questioning, "How is it with you, lady?" One moment more and the passion that made a corpse of *Polonius* might have wreaked vengeance on the guilty *Queen;* for though *Hamlet* declares that he is neither splenitive nor rash, yet is there "something dangerous" in him, a something that might have led him to strangle *Laertes* had he lost entire self-control. That the *Queen* believes her son capable of the deed is seen at the opening of this scene, when *Hamlet* says: —

> "Come, come, and sit you down; you shall not budge;
>    You go not, till I set you up a glass
>    Where you may see the inmost part of you."

These are not desperate words, and yet the *Queen* cries out : —

> " What wilt thou do ?  Thou wilt not *murder* me ?
> Help, help, ho ! "

Killing the *Queen* was not impossible to the *Hamlet* of Fechter, who was convinced of her complicity in his father's murder.

> " O Hamlet ! speak no more ,
> Thou turn'st mine eyes into my very soul ;
> And there I see such black and grainéd spots
> As will not leave their tinct."

Mere marriage with a brother-in-law, even after two months of widowhood, hardly admits of so fearful a confession ; and her fear of being murdered by *Hamlet*, leads to the inference that she knows she deserves the punishment.   Further coloring for this hypothesis may be obtained in *Hamlet's* response to the *Ghost* : —

> " Do not look upon me ;
> Lest, with this piteous action you convert
> My stern effects ; then what have I to do
> Will want true colors ; tears, perchance, for blood."

Surely this does not indicate absence of will on *Hamlet's* part ; and as stage ghosts always produce the effect they desire, the dead king attains the purpose of his " pale glaring."   Certainly he had no such tearful influence over *Hamlet* during the first interview. Is the object, then, the same ?   Indeed it would seem not ; and since I find Shakespeare so ready to agree with Fechter, I doubt my ability to withhold allegiance to this startling innovation.

The critic may one day entertain one opinion of

*Hamlet,* and another the next ; he may be very positive in some particulars, and not quite sure in others. He can leave a door open by which his opinions may make a dignified exit, should an intellectual breeze threaten to overthrow them ; but the actor enjoys no such privilege. He must thoroughly understand his intentions before being able to interpret them. He must feel certain that, according to his light, his conception is right, or he cannot render it with force or send conviction to the hearts and heads of his audience. The business of the critic, therefore, in this matter of " Hamlet," is not so much with the conception of the character as with the manner in which the actor's conception is carried out. If it is consistent from beginning to end, if it takes such strong hold as to prevent any escape from it, if its great power absolutely bullies one out of cherished theories, if its humanity makes one look back upon previous *Hamlets* as so many lay-figures galvanized into spasmodic action, if it absorbs attention and creates a positive sensation, then does the actor merit critical enthusiasm ; for the critic's business is to *appreciate,* to appreciate is to estimate justly, and just estimation calls for as much delight at what is fine as disapprobation of what is false. Fechter produced all these effects. He was great not only in his originality but in his rendering, the greatness of which I will do my poor best to show by photographing his *Hamlet* in such details as are food for critics and actors.

Fechter's study was not confined to his own part, as was seen immediately in the reading of *Horatio,* upon the entrance of the *Ghost :* —

> " But, soft; behold ! lo, where it comes again !
> I'll cross it, though it blast me.   Stay, illusion !
> If thou hast any sound, or use of voice,
> Speak to me.   (*Ghost stops.*)"

In Pre-Fechterian days *Horatios* senselessly *crossed
the Ghost's path*, as if such a step would stay its pro-
gress.   Not so with Fechter, whose *Horatio* made the
sign of the cross, at which the *Ghost* stopped as a
Catholic ghost should.   Once interpreted thus, intelligence exclaims " Of course ! " and yet *Horatios* have
been crossing the stage for three hundred years !

He was gloomy enough, was Fechter's *Hamlet*, as
he sat beside his mother, — starting when the *King* addressed him as " our *son*," yet gently exclaiming while
kissing the *Queen's* hand with courtly grace, and giving
by almost imperceptible accent a key to the estimate
in which he held his uncle-father,

> "I shall in all my best obey *you*, madam."

Left to himself, he gazed fondly at his father's portrait,
worn about his neck, and illustrated the beautiful apostrophe by reference to it.   Thus did Fechter prepare
his audience for the text.   Misunderstanding was impossible.   His *Hamlet* deceived no one.   He was as
honest as the day is light.   He drew his lines plainly
between friend and acquaintance, and his fondness for
*Horatio* was strongly defined from the moment of meeting.   There were three distinct shades of tone in " My
good friend " (meaning *Horatio*), " I am very glad to
see you " (meaning *Marcellus*), and " Good even, sir "
(meaning *Bernardo*).   *Hamlet* wasted no affection.

He was generous; but he was losing faith in mankind, and trusted few.

An expression of great and tender beauty passed over Fechter's face as, with clasped hands, he murmured

" My father, — methinks I see my father ; "

while there was filial pride in his explanation, with hand upon *Horatio's* shoulder,

" He was a *man ;* take him for all in all,
I shall not look upon his like again."

When *Horatio* described his encounter with the *Ghost,* Fechter crossed his hands the moment his father was mentioned, as if praying for the unhappy spirit. The action was entirely natural to a Catholic. Appealingly sweet was his

"Did you not speak to it?"

addressed to *Marcellus*, to which his *Horatio* replied,

" My lord, *I* did."

Doubting, not willing to believe without strong evidence, he gave the line, " Then saw you not his face?" as if it read " Then you did *not* see his face ; " which seems reasonable from *Horatio's* answer : —

"O yes, my lord, he wore his beaver up.
. . . . . . .
*Hamlet.* I would *I* had been there.
*Horatio.* It would have much amazed you.
*Hamlet.* Very like, very like."

These lines have always been given as a response to *Horatio.* Fechter, meditating on the startling intelligence that the apparition wore *his beaver up*, murmured " Very like," as if the sentence read, " Very like — my father." Of course the *Ghost* would amaze *Hamlet*. He is already amazed,— therefore the " very like " fits far more gracefully into Fechter's setting. Tears filled his eyes as he asked,

> " Stayed it long ? "

When *Hamlet, Horatio,* and *Marcellus* appear in the fourth scene, Fechter caused *Hamlet* to come from an opposite direction. Why? Because he had previously said that he would visit them " upon the platform, 'twixt eleven and twelve." They meet for the first time, and the dialogue says as much. Strange that it took a Frenchman to find this out.

Enveloped in a gray picturesque cloak and black velvet cowl, Fechter's *Hamlet* dropped the former, and, with hands on *Horatio* at sight of the *Ghost*, delivered the invocation with solemn tender earnestness, removing the cowl at the word *king*, and throwing a filial pathos into *father*.

> " Go on, *I*'ll follow thee."

His exit was slow, but in no way unnaturally measured, — with sword unsheathed and held in the left hand as if it were a cross.

> " Alas, *poor* ghost ! "

was given with pitying sweetness of tone. Kneeling at the words, " I *am* thy father's spirit," Fechter did not rise until the adjuration, " Haste me to know," etc. ; and though his back was turned to the audience during the *Ghost's* confession, there was much expression in his pantomime. Nevertheless, but for the exceedingly clever management of the *Ghost's* instantaneous disappearance, — the invention being Fechter's, — it was a pity to lose the play of feature which Fechter could have thrown into his eager, listening silence. He bowed profoundly at the *Ghost's*, "Fare thee well at once!" and when *Horatio* called without, "Heaven secure him!" meaning *Hamlet*, Fechter, intent upon the *Ghost*, prayerfully added "So be it," — turning the words to a deeper significance than they had ever possessed. What immediately followed was no less admirably treated. *Horatio* alone was his valued friend, *Horatio* alone had so far sworn not to reveal the news, and *Hamlet* hurriedly began to tell his story, "There's ne'er a villain dwelling in all Denmark," — when, suddenly remembering and doubting *Marcellus*, he turned from his purpose and added, "but he's an arrant knave;" at which platitude *Horatio* has reason to criticise his friend. The line,

"You, as your business and desire shall point you,"

was addressed to *Marcellus*. *Hamlet's* "wild and whirling" words were because of his presence. He was talking to conceal thought. Taking *Horatio's* hand ·(according to stage direction) he remarked to him,

"Touching this vision here, —
It is an honest ghost, that let me tell you."

Then, looking at *Marcellus*, he continued,

"For *your* desire to know what is between us,
O'ermaster it as you may."

Fechter's *Hamlet* did not insult *Horatio* by assuming superior wisdom and exclaiming, "There are more things in heaven and earth, Horatio, than are dreamt of in *your* philosophy," but accented *philosophy*, by which the pronoun possessed the same significance as when Edmund Kean substituted *our* for *your*.

With arm linked in *Horatio's*, *Hamlet* said, "Let us go in together," and leaving *Marcellus* down the stage addressed to him the parting injunction, "And still your fingers on your lips, I pray." The line is certainly intended for *Marcellus*, who cannot be included in *Hamlet's* invitation, inasmuch as, after the exit, *Hamlet* must impart the *Ghost's* secret to *Horatio*, the two friends not meeting again until the third act, when *Hamlet*, in referring to the play, says, —

> "One scene of it comes near the circumstance
> Which I have told *thee*, of my father's death."

If circumstantial evidence proves aught, it proves the truth of Fechter's conception. There was no ranting in his rendering of the couplet,

> "The time is out of joint," etc.

Its power was in its concentrated desperation.

The admirable shades and touches in the second act were equally pertinent. Dialogue never received more varied or more thoughtful treatment. *Polonius* never attempted to master such keen madness. "Conception is a blessing; but as your daughter may conceive, — friend, look to 't." It was a mad laugh that followed "friend." *Hamlet* pointed to his open book as he muttered, "look to 't;" and *Polonius*, literal in all things, ran his eye over the page to learn the "cause of this defect." *Hamlet* watched him narrowly, as if to see how the simulated madness took effect, when the old man delivered his side speech beginning, "How pregnant sometimes his replies are!" and there was a world of weariness pent up in his reiterated exclamation, "Except my life!" Tired, tired, tired! Revenge and sorrow were never nature's heritage to such as he. Too brave, too conscientious to shake duty off, relief was sought in word and expression.

*Hamlet's* reception of *Rosencrantz* and *Guildenstern* was most cordial, until he saw his uncle's portrait around the neck of the latter; then expression and manner changed, and the question, "Were you not sent for?" was put eagerly, with suspicion of foul play which waxed stronger as he bade them speak "to the purpose." Words mean something when thus interpreted. *Hamlet's* rejoinder, "And those that would make mouths at him while my father lived, give twenty, forty, fifty, an hundred ducats apiece for his picture in little," was illustrated by his taking up the picture pendent from *Guildenstern's* neck. Upon dropping it, he crossed to the right, and made an "aside," perfectly comprehensible to all, of the succeeding sentence, "There is something in this more than natural, if philosophy could find it out." Were audiences given to acute criticism, and did reason rule the day, theatres would resound with bravos at such renderings as this, rather than at the tearing of passion to tatters.

One knew by the tender music of *Hamlet's* voice in exclaiming, "O Jephthah, Judge of Israel, what a treasure hadst thou ! " that his thoughts were with " the fair Ophelia," and it was this memory that rendered him so gentle in checking *Polonius* for interrupting the player.    Hushing him, commanding silence by putting finger on lips with as much kindliness as if the old courtier were indeed a big baby, *Hamlet* took up the text, " So ; proceed you," and for the first time the little word *so* was set in its proper action.    *Hamlet* listened with such interest to the *Actor's* speech as to accompany it with unconscious pantomine and silent repetition of the words ; but this was not original with Fechter, Garrick having done the same.

"But who, ah, woe ! had seen the mobled queen."

" The mobled queen ! " repeated Fechter's *Hamlet*, thinking of his mother ; and, struck by the coincidence, became so absorbed as to leave *Polonius* unchecked when he again interrupted the *First Actor*.    There was genuine respectful sympathy in *Hamlet's* manner of instructing that the players be well treated ; such sympathy as, if prevalent in society, would raise the stage to its proper level, — beside the pulpit.    Equally wonderful in its humanity was the pity breathing through *Hamlet's* command to the first actor, that *Polonius* be not mocked.

The tremendous soliloquy closing this act was marvellous in variety.    Its gradual crescendo and diminuendo were most artistic, while the climax,

" The play 's the thing,
Wherein I 'll catch the conscience of the King."

came like a sudden revelation to a tortured brain, and
was clutched at (if I may say so) with all the energy
with which nature seizes upon forlorn hopes.

Fechter pointed the moral of the soliloquy, "To be
or not to be," by bringing on an unsheathed sword, as
if he had again been contemplating the suicide that
would free him from his oath.

Very beautiful and equally original was *Hamlet's*
scene with *Ophelia*. He was a lover the moment his
eyes fell upon her, and he cast aside every semblance
of madness until *Ophelia* returned his letters, when the
change of Fechter's expression was as great as the
change of language ; but when listening to the gentle
maiden's reproaches, there was pictured such agonized
regret, at throwing away every chance of happiness, as
made the heart ache, for Fechter's *Hamlet* was always
real, always a suffering man, never an actor.

How pantomine illuminates a sentence was seen
in *Hamlet's* reference to the power of Beauty, which
"will sooner transform Honesty from what it is to a
bawd, than the force of Honesty can translate Beauty
into his likeness ; this was sometimes a paradox," —
here Fechter paused, looked sadly at the letters in his
hand returned by the woman *Hamlet* loved, and then
added, — "but *now* the time gives it proof." Still his
heart was bursting to speak the truth, and the confession, "I did love you once," was given with tearful
eyes and choked utterance. When *Ophelia* exclaimed,
"I was the more deceived," Fechter's tender action,
unseen by her, denoted that he *must* fold her in his
arms ; but, forced to restraint, he honestly, earnestly

begged her to get to a nunnery, as the only sanctuary worthy of her. Then seeing *Polonius*, he, to test *Ophelia's* truthfulness, asked, " Where 's your father? " and, finding her false, burst into frenzied raving, intended far more for the ears of her father than for the helpless creature trembling before him. Again subdued by love, *Hamlet* approached *Ophelia* with extended arms, almost embraced her, but, recollecting that he was watched by *Polonius*, cried pathetically, " To a nunnery, go," and, thoroughly overcome, rushed off the stage. In this scene Fechter did not allow *Hamlet* to see the *King*, for this espionage would so convince him of his uncle's guilt as to render the play unnecessary.

Nothing could be finer of its kind than Fechter's intelligent and colloquial delivery of *Hamlet's* advice to the players ; and in this connection it should be stated that he was the first to introduce a boy with chopins, in lieu of a woman actress.[1]

Hamlet gazed fondly at *Ophelia* when announcing the Court's coming to the play, showing first the lover before putting on the mask.

" I eat the air, promise-crammed ; you cannot feed capons so," said *Hamlet*.

" I have nothing with this answer, Hamlet ; these words are not mine," rejoined the *King*.

" No, nor mine, now ; " and Fechter, by an exquisite action of the hand, made you see why those words were

[1] It may be said of Fechter, as Hazlitt said of Kean, that if Shakespeare had written marginal directions to the players, in the manner of German dramatists, he would often have directed them to do what Fechter did.

no longer his. They had passed into the air for all time, and belonged to space. Pantomime has its prose and its poetry. This action was rhythmic.

He never forgot to spare *Polonius* in the presence of others. " I did enact Julius Cæsar," maunders the old man. " I was killed i' the capital; Brutus killed me."

" It was a brute part of him," *Hamlet* replied, and then, walking away, added as an aside, " to kill so capital a calf there." The very word *there* suggests this treatment of the sentence, and yet again Fechter discovered it.

" Nay, then, let the Devil wear black, for I 'll have a suit of sables," reads the customary text; but what said Fechter? " Let the Devil wear black 'fore *I* 'll have a suit of sable." The mystery is solved at once, and, turning to the Folio Shakespeare, the line is so written down. As the Folio is supposed to have been printed from a playhouse copy, Fechter's version was probably as correct as it was intelligible.

> " *Ophelia.* 'T is brief, my lord.
> *Hamlet.* As woman's love."

Most *Hamlets* insult *Ophelia* by hurling this reply at her. Fechter gave it as if communing with his own thoughts, and looked the while toward his mother. " That 's wormwood," was addressed to *Horatio ;* and, " If she should break it now," to *King* and *Queen.*

Admirable was Fechter's action after the discovery and call for " lights." Throughout the play *Hamlet* had lain at *Ophelia's* feet, but had *amused* himself (so reads the conventional stage business) with nothing, not even with the specified fan. Before him lay the text of the play, which he followed closely, thus anticipating it and watching the effect upon the royal pair. Discovery made and audience gone, Fechter tore the leaves from his play-book and scattered them in the air, as he rose and delivered the well-known quatrain. His utterance was rapid ; excitement at last rendered it thick. The blood rushed to his head, he put his hand to his throat as if choking. " Ah, ha ! " became a gasp ; he leaned upon *Horatio* and, for relief, for solace, called for music. There was no bridging over an inexplicable chasm, such as we have seen from childhood. It was perfect nature. Upon the entrance of *Guildenstern* and *Rosencrantz*, *Hamlet* fell into a chair from exhaustion, until his mother's name was mentioned, when, out of that courtesy which was rarely forgotten, he rose.

*Guildenstern*, with the locket about his neck, was far more hateful to *Hamlet* than the less treacherous *Rosencrantz.*

" *Hamlet.* Sir, I cannot.

" *Guildenstern.* What, my lord ?

" *Hamlet.* Make you a wholesome answer ; . . . but, sir, such answer as I can make, you shall command ; or rather, as you say, my mother ; therefore, no more, but to the matter : my mother, you say —

" *Rosencrantz.* Then, thus she says : your behavior hath struck her into amazement and admiration."

Here *Hamlet* snubbed *Guildenstern*, and " my mother, you say," was addressed to *Rosencrantz*, who immediately took up the thread of argument as shown. Hazlitt declares that acting *Hamlet* is like the attempt to embody a shadow. He would never have made this statement had he seen Fechter's key to the character.

The whole scene with the *Queen* was one panorama of tragic pictures. Having killed *Polonius*, Fechter elaborated Shakespeare's few words by the agony of his expression at having made so fatal a mistake, and by throwing away his sword that it might not be repeated.

The excitement produced by the *Ghost's* appearance yielded to regret at his departure ; and there was also a tenderness toward his guilty mother, who finally knelt before him, being raised up gently at the words, " Confess yourself to Heaven," etc. When *Hamlet* bade her good-night, she attempted to bless him, but was firmly, not unkindly, repelled. This action was followed by the lines,

> " And when you are desirous to *be* blessed,
> I 'll blessing beg of *you*."

Before the sobbing *Queen* retired, she once more turned to her son, exclaiming, " Hamlet " (this was Fechter's introduction), and stretched out her hands for a filial embrace. *Hamlet* held up his father's picture, the sight of which spoke volumes to the wretched woman, who staggered from the stage. Kissing this picture, *Hamlet* murmured sadly,

> " I must be cruel, only to be kind ; "

then, taking light in hand and raising the arras, gazed at *Polonius*, exclaiming,

> " Thus bad begins, and worse remains behind."

After the third act *Hamlet* is but half his former self. The actor would willingly stop short, leaving the last two acts to the imagination, and in the present condition of stock companies the critic would gladly assent to curtailment; but it must be five acts or nothing, and patience endures to the last. Fechter's treatment of the *King*, in the fourth act, was that of undisguised contempt. " If your messenger find him [*Polonius*] not there [in heaven], seek him in the other place *yourself;*" and it was seen that if *Hamlet* were not guarded, he would then and there have sent the *King* to "the other place" in search of his courtier.

When Fechter produced " Hamlet " in his own theatre, the time of the churchyard scene was that of a brilliant sunset, making a fine contrast between the thoughtless joy of nature and the grief of humanity. Moreover, it is neither customary nor practicable to dig graves by the fickle light of the moon feebly assisted by one small lantern; and when truth is compatible with art, — for my part, I believe the two walk hand in hand, — it should be adhered to. Fechter's apostrophe to *poor* Yorick was singularly tender : " Here hung those lips, that I have kissed I know not how oft ; " and Fechter carried the skull almost to his lips, when he put it away with a shiver. From time immemorial *Ophelia's* body has been borne from *church* to churchyard, when the text tells us that her burial in sanctified ground is granted under protest.

> " She is allowed her virgin crants,
> Her maiden strewments, and the bringing home
> Of bell and burial.
>
> .    .    .    .    .    .    .    .    .

We should profane the service of the dead
To sing a requiem, and such rest to her
As to peace-parted souls."

Hence Fechter caused *Ophelia* to be brought through the churchyard gateway, and the officiating priest wore none of the insignia of his office.

" What, the fair Ophelia ? "

and, overwhelmed with agony, *Hamlet* fell on his knees beside a tomb and buried his face in his hands. In the controversy between *Hamlet* and *Laertes*, Macready and Kemble leaped into the grave, and there went through the grappling in true Punch and Judy fashion. The illustrious example has been often followed ; but Fechter wisely abstained from the absurdity, not approaching the grave until his last word was spoken, when, gazing in agony at the gaping void and at *Ophelia's* corse, he was dragged off the stage by *Horatio.*

In the art of fencing Fechter was consummate ; consequently the final scene was full of spirit and interest. His arrangement of the stage was likewise admirable. In the background ran a gallery, to which a short flight of stairs led on each side of the stage, and by which all exits and entrances were made. To the left stood the throne, where sat the *King.* The moment *Hamlet* exclaimed,

" Ho ! let the door be locked.
Treachery ! seek it out."

the *King* exhibited signs of fear ; and, while *Laertes* made his terrible confession, the regicide stole to the opposite stairs, shielding himself from *Hamlet's* observation behind a group of courtiers, who, paralyzed with horror, failed to remark the action. *Laretes* no sooner uttered the words, "The King's to blame," than *Hamlet* turned suddenly to the throne in search of his victim. Discovering the ruse, he rushed up the left-hand stairs, met the *King* in the centre of the gallery, and stabbed him. It would be difficult to conceive a more effective manner of despatching *Claudius,* or one more in harmony with good taste. He was not butchered as in the old "business," and the stage was relieved of one dead body. As he descended the stairs the potent poison stole upon *Hamlet,* who, murmuring "The rest is silence," fell dead on the corpse of *Laertes,* thus showing his forgiveness of treachery and remembrance of *Ophelia.* There was no contortion in Fechter's manner of dying. Edmund Kean was no doubt right in illustrating a death by poison ; but if *Hamlet* dies thus, surely *Laertes* must meet his doom in like manner. Two such exhibitions would be beyond human endurance ; and, as *Laertes* dies first, *Hamlet's* effects would be lost. Therefore Fechter was not without reason in abstaining from literalness.

Does not the photograph, dim as it is, show Fechter's power in Hamlet? Does it not give evidence of ideas and ideality?

The fair hair of Fechter's *Hamlet* was not an original conception, though from the criticisms one might have imagined as much. Goethe declares that "as a Dane, as a Northman, Hamlet is fair-haired and blue-eyed by descent." "Absurd !" cries a voice ; "how is this possible, when we are distinctly told that his father's hair is 'sable silvered'?" Does it follow that *Hamlet* the younger must therefore be dark haired? To my way of thinking, Fechter, when he first arrived in this country, gave us the ideal *Hamlet*, who, with all his manly beauty, "is fat and scant of breath." "Brown-complexioned people in their youth are seldom plump," argues Goethe. Fechter was thoroughly manly, as *Hamlet*, who is much given to exercise, should be. No contrary opinion can take comfort in *Hamlet's* declaration, that *Claudius* is no more like his father than he to Hercules; for Hercules performed such feats of prowess as astounded both gods and men. Fechter was robust without being unpleasantly so; he was graceful, supple as an athlete, courtly, wondrously picturesque; and his beautiful flaxen wig so transformed his coloring as to cause his dark-hazel eyes to be mistaken for blue.

There has been something said of Fechter's liberties with Shakespeare's language. Curious to know how much truth lay in this accusation, I have followed him, while acting, with book in hand. Fechter spoke no more than was set down to him, — nor less. He was what is called, in stage parlance, "letter perfect." There were a few trips of accent, — very few, — made with the lips entirely; for when the offending passages were afterwards shown to Fechter, he spoke them correctly, showing that the head had not been at fault. And here lies the secret of the charge that Fechter had no settled convictions as to the reading of *Hamlet*. Rarely repeating the *same* error, he supplemented it with another, — as, for example,

"O horrible, horrible, most *horrible!*"

intending " *most* horrible," and so delivering the passage on the following performance. These were slight blemishes to weigh against a beautiful work of art.

> " When reason yields to passion's wild alarms,
>     And the whole state of man is up in arms,
>     What but a critic would condemn the player
>     For pausing here, when cool sense pauses there ?
>     Whilst, working from the heart, the fire I trace,
>     And mark it strongly flaming to the face ;
>     Whilst in each sound I hear the very man,
>     *I can't catch words, and pity those who can.*"

Nor is there much more foundation for the accusation of " cutting " Shakespeare. No actor has ever spoken the whole of *Hamlet*. Betterton took many liberties ; and what Garrick did finally shall be referred to. When the latter performed this character in Dublin, an Irish critic suggested the advisability of his leaving out *Hamlet's* " abominable " soliloquy while the *King* is at prayers. Garrick carried out the suggestion, and not until recently has it been restored to English theatres. Fechter's version was that of Kemble and of the stage. If, in the last act, he did not always deliver the frenzied speech addressed to *Laertes*, and cut short his dying words, it was because of exceptional circumstances.

Whether there ever lived a thoroughly satisfactory *Hamlet* is extremely doubtful. What Burbage was, nobody knows. What Betterton made of the character it is possible to conceive ; for, with all Cibber's praise of this actor, Quin owned that he " would not go down in Garrick's days," — and as Quin himself, grounded on

Booth's and Betterton's school, died artistically as soon
as Garrick's genius illuminated the English stage, the
critic has very grave doubts as to any standard set up
by Cibber, who showed his bad taste by cordially hating Garrick's acting. Then as to Garrick's *Hamlet*, it
comes in " questionable shape ; " for, though the great
little man was the first to produce the play in 1742,
shorn of every objectionable word and the traditional
music, he gave the address to the players like a peda-
gogue, — walked backward and forward, twirling a white
*handkerchief,* while exclaiming,

" Some must laugh, while some must weep,"

and performed other antics hardly compatible with
Shakespeare's *Dane*. That he failed to appreciate
the character is evident from the manner in which
he slaughtered the play thirty years after, when he
" improved " Shakespeare out of sight in the last acts,
and contemplated turning the grave-diggers and *Osric*,
" the Danish macaroni," into a farce ! Yet this " mass
of deformity " held the stage eight years with a *Hamlet* that exemplified the theory of perpetual motion !
Cooke in *Hamlet* was " one mass of awkward error ; " neither does Kemble, nor does the elder Kean,
owe his fame to his personation of the character.
Knowing this, Fechter acquires additional respect for
his rendition of *Hamlet*.

Possessing good height, small hands and feet, a face
so like Garrick's in contour and complexion as in a
Garrick wig to render the resemblance astonishing, and
so wonderful in expression as, like Talma's to need but

the passing of a hand to transform broad comedy into deepest tragedy; with a large magnetic ever-changing hazel eye, with pantomime that rivalled Ristori's, with a rich melodious voice that ran the gamut of the passions, with abundant sentiment and humor equally developed, with a sculptor's knowledge of form, a painter's love of costume and color, and a Frenchman's education in the best school of acting, Fechter took his place among the few great actors of the world. With regard to his pronunciation of English there was really very little fault to be found. In private it rarely occurred to the most careful listeners that Fechter was not, so far as concerns accent, an Englishman. On the stage, however, there were times when, if he did not feel well, his speech became thick, or when, if carried away by passion, his delivery was somewhat indistinct; but ordinarily his enunciation was wonderfully clear and his English far purer than that spoken by the actors around him. It is somewhat amusing to hear Americans, who are proverbially inelegant in their language, finding fault with Fechter's occasional slips of the tongue. What would they say to Garrick, with his *shupreme, shuperior, vurtue, fersely* (for fiercely), *Isrel* for Israel, *villin* for villain, and *appeal* for appall? Churchill, in his " Rosciad," declared that " Garrick never did or never could speak ten successive lines of Shakespeare with grammatical propriety." Nevertheless Garrick was great. What would they say to Kemble's " foggy throat," that was wont to

" Fill all thy bones with a-ches,"

and whose vitiated orthoepy induced Leigh Hunt to publish a lexicon, that theatre-goers might have a key to the text? The elder Kean had countless vulgarisms of pronunciation. Vulgarity is inexcusable. A foreign accent may not be desirable, yet it is far more grateful to a musical ear than the common variety of nasal twang in which both our pulpit and stage indulge to an intolerable extent.

Writer, as well as sculptor and actor, Fechter was the author of French plays to which he never appended his name, as well as of several English dramatizations. No mean poet, he rendered " Romeo and Juliet " into French verse.

" Hence, to thy praises," Fechter, " I agree,
And pleased with nature must be pleased with thee!"

# FECHTER'S

# "CLAUDE MELNOTTE."

# FECHTER'S "CLAUDE MELNOTTE."

———◆———

OF the popularity of maudlin sentimentality there
can be no doubt ; otherwise the "Lady of Lyons"
would long since have been consigned to an early
grave with never a headstone to mark it. Thriving
like a green bay-tree, it brings forth fruit even in chill
December, breathing, apparently, no other atmosphere
than that of its own tropical passion. To deny its
cleverness as an acting play is as absurd as to deny its
bathos ; yet, clever though it be in effects, no one but
Charles Fechter ever elevated it out of its drivel into
romance. In reality *Claude Melnotte* is a "cad." He
lies like a dozen troopers, he appropriates other people's
rings and snuff-boxes, he pretends to be a gentleman.
After undergoing a grand moral reform by taking
part in the French spoliation of Italy, he returns to
woo his wife, and establishes his title to the privilege
by paying his father-in-law's debts with the silver
spoons, "old masters," and *objets d'art* stolen from
pillaged palaces. A fine record, surely.

Had *Melnotte* served in our civil war, the press would
have united in one prolonged howl over the infamy of
such vandalism ; but the glamour of the footlights stifles
the expostulations of conscience, and Fechter, despising

Bulwer's character while appreciating the effectiveness of the play, lifted *Melnotte* out of his very self and made a hero of him.    If this is not creation, what is it? Men and women, girls and boys, old maids and bachelors, were spellbound.    Hating *Pauline* for not immediately surrendering at discretion, they lived over past or dreamed of future joys.    An effect like this renders actor far greater than play and proves the magic of real art, without which mock sentiment is — mock sentiment.

English journals pronounced Fechter's *Melnotte* the best that had ever been seen, and the verdict was doubtless correct, notwithstanding that Macready first brought out the " Lady of Lyons " at Covent Garden Theatre in 1838.    With all Macready's ability — and that he was great in *Werner, Virginius, Richelieu, Lear,* and *William Tell,* no one who values the opinions of the best critics of a past generation can doubt — he did not shine as a lover.    He invested his mistress with no reflected glory.    He did his duty to the situation and text ; and, doing but this, deprived passion of its sentiment.    Love drops " like the gentle rain from heaven," and has no more to do with duty than the north pole has to do with the equator.    " Mr. Macready's *Claude,*" says the *London Times,* " was a less youthful and a more staid, serious, and — using the phrase without suggestion of offence — 'stilted person.' "

Undisturbed by the conventionalities of the English stage, desirous of putting as much nature as possible into the play, Fechter suggested several alterations to Bulwer, who, acknowledging their propriety, made them without demur. The most important of these were the suppression of the first scene, by which condensation the play was strengthened ; the substitution of *Beauseant* in person for the letter formerly delivered to and read by *Melnotte ;* the omission of the extra lines after the words " Do you ? " at the end of the second act ; and the conclusion of the play at *Melnotte's* exclamation, " Thy husband ! " by which artistic curtailment the curtain fell upon the exciting tableau of *Pauline* rushing to her husband's arms. After seeing this finale Bulwer himself marvelled that he had never thought of it. *Melnotte's* soliloquy in the fourth act was shorn of the lines :

> " She wakes to scorn, to hate, but not to shudder
> Beneath the touch of my abhorred love."

Costume and business underwent a greater revolution. Instead of the blouse and trousers worn by Macready and his successors, Fechter donned a rich bourgeois dress of the period, such as a " village prince " would be likely to wear at a festival. Instead of a nondescript uniform, Hessians, and cocked hat in the second act, Fechter wore powdered hair, and put on the black court suit, silk stockings, and chapeau bras of an Italian prince, who had nothing whatever to do with the plain hair and plain clothes of the revolution. Instead of concealing himself in the last act behind the feathers of a hypothetical hat, Fechter was disguised by his own hair and a mustache, and stood with a table between *Pauline* and himself, she not daring to raise her eyes to the man who is supposed to be *Melnotte's* intimate friend.

Prior to this interview, Fechter overcame the exceedingly awkward position in which the dramatist places *Melnotte*, — in introducing him to the *Deschappelles* and then leaving him for five or eight minutes with never a soul to talk to, and without a reason for such unwarrantable incivility, — by indicating that he would in no way disturb the drawing up of the marriage contract, and by retiring to a conservatory where he was presented by *Damas* to various ladies and gentlemen. An unnatural situation was thus rendered perfectly *comme il faut*, and all by the substitution of an evening assembly of interested friends for an afternoon meeting of the *Deschappelles* family.

*Claude Melnotte* is a Frenchman, and Fechter treated him as such. The moment he appeared, with prize rifle in hand, the audience felt the passion of the lover and longed to see the object of his homage. Poetic even in details, Fechter straightway laid his gun not on table or chair or in a corner, after the manner of ordinary *Melnottes*, but on the edge of his · easel, beneath the portrait of *Pauline*, making of it a votive offering to the idol of his heart. How much this trifle meant ! From first to last he treated his mother with downright affection. This in itself was a revelation, — stage mothers being regarded by their heroic children as necessary evils, to be tolerated with cold indifference. Hope, indignation, revenge, were vividly portrayed in the first act ; while Fechter's comedy, in the second act, was good acting, for it *was* acting, — as far removed from Fechter's real comedy as artifice is removed from reality. His *Melnotte* was acting a part which he despised, and there was consequently a want of repose about it quite in sympathy with the situation ; but he took snuff nonchalantly, and occasionally put his hands in his pockets, as nobility always did during the reign of *petits maîtres.* Left alone with *Pauline,* constraint disappeared before the magic of love ; and in his mouth the picture of that "palace lifting to eternal summer " became true art, fully justifying *Pauline's* tribute to his " eloquent tongue." We listened to sound, not sense, and saw the vision of love's young dream ; and for the first time we saw *Melnotte* do justice to Bulwer's intention. The passage,

> " If thou wouldst have me paint
> The home to which, could love fulfil its prayers,
> This hand would lead thee, — listen,"

received proper treatment. "Could love fulfil its prayers " was spoken sadly, after a pause, and almost as an aside ; nor did *Melnotte* fold *Pauline* in his arms until he was warmed by the recitation of his fancy. Very charming was the business at the end of this act, when *Melnotte,* seated at the right, overcome with agony at the treacherous part he was playing, and resting his arm upon the table beside him, gazed with fond remorse into *Pauline's* face as she stole toward him and stroked the extended hand. The tableau on *Pauline's* exit was admirable, and, when the curtain fell, *Melnotte* stood out as the picture of melancholy abstraction.

But it was in the third and fourth acts that Fechter showed his power, in the manliness of his passionate atonement. Picturesque and noble in his black velvet suit and gray cloak, he made *Beauseant* and *Glavis* shrink from his dangerous presence as jackals shrink from the lion. His exclamation, " O Heaven, forgive me ! " when wrapping *Pauline* in his cloak he led her to *Melnotte's* cottage, was the very keynote of despair. He put his neatest art into the scene of *Melnotte's* self-abasement. There was no raving. The confession beginning :

> " Pauline, by pride
> Angels have fallen ere thy time,"

was rendered with " a magic to exorcise hate," and culminated with a truly beautiful and original point.

> " And when thou art happy, and hast half forgot
> Him who so loved, so wronged thee, think at least
> Heaven left some remnant of the angels still
> In that poor peasant's nature !
> Ha ! my mother !
>
> [*Widow comes down stairs ;*]"

says the play-book.

Now, what did Fechter ? Instead of summoning his mother as if she were a lackey, this admirable artist completely transfigured words and situation. At the beginning of the sentence quoted, the *Widow* appeared at the upper door, quietly descended the stairs, and stood beside her son, when, heart-broken he exclaimed,

> " *Ah !* my mother ! "

and threw himself into her arms to find relief in tears. This alteration should be adopted by future *Claudes*. Equally fine was Fechter's expression at the close of the act, as he followed *Pauline's* exit with his eyes, and sinking to the ground, invoked Heaven's blessing upon her.

In wonderful contrast with the quiet beauty of the third was Fechter's finale to the fourth act. The worn-out text was clothed anew. It was a real scene, a real parting. The audience was thrilled by *Melnotte's* noble passion ; the blood tingled through their veins as if they were being charged with electricity. The divine spark, of which we hear so much and see so little, asserted its presence ; and when the curtain fell upon an entirely new tableau, no one could resist the enthusiasm of re-calling again and again him who had made a magnifi-cent hero out of an old stage bore. To the last there was manifest *Claude's* love for his mother, which so justifies the *Widow's* adoration of her son. He would not hurt her by even a word. After *Melnotte's* exclama-tion, "the husband of a being so beautiful . . . may be low born," Fechter took his mother's hand, adding, "there is no guilt in the decrees of Providence," with a tenderness that made us ask, "Why can't we have more acting like it?" His last embrace was for this widowed mother, and at sight of so true a son, so great a lover, even the manliest eye sympathized with rough *Colonel Damas* as he murmured, "I'll be hanged if I'm not going to blubber!"

The Marseillaise is usually played at the close of this act. Fechter introduced it after *Damas's* declara-tion that *Melnotte* would make an excellent soldier. Beginning *pianissimo*, the grand hymn rose to a gradual *crescendo* until the climax, when it burst forth with all its force. After such a vivid scene, of course the fifth act, in which *Melnotte* does little more than "stand at ease," was comparatively tame ; but the old glow came over us in watching Fechter's facial expression during the short interview with *Pauline*, in the final action of the tearing of the contract, and the happy embrace of man and wife with which Fechter rightly terminated the play.

" All the world loves a lover," says Emerson, and in this poetic fact lay Fechter's greatest power. Fechter's love-making was so far removed from what is seen on the stage, that the sympathetic spectator forgot its fiction. And it was because of this ideal element in his lovers that Fechter found his greatest admirers among women. Possessed of more sentiment than men, and hungry for sympathy, they recognized " the triumph of woman " in Fechter's *Ruy Blas* and *Claude Melnotte,* and were grateful to the artist.

# FECHTER

# IN FOUR CHARACTERS.

———◆——— •

*Frédéric de Marsan,*

"ON DEMANDE UN GOUVERNEUR."

*Don Çæsar de Bazan,*

"DON CÆSAR DE BAZAN."

*Fabien and Louis dei Franchi,*

"CORSICAN BROTHERS."

*Monte Cristo,*

"MONTE CRISTO."

# "FRÉDÉRIC DE MARSAN."

VERSATILE, as the highest order of dramatic talent must ever be in order to sound the chord of human feeling, Fechter was equally at home in low comedy, high comedy, melodrama, and tragedy. Whatever he did last seemed that for which he was best fitted. His *Frédéric de Marsan* in the little French comedy of "On Demande un Gouverneur" was the perfection of neat acting. Never once did he raise his voice above a colloquial tone, not once did he make any greater effort for points than he would have made in his own drawing-room; yet, by merely holding the mirror up to nature, he riveted attention as closely as in the most effective dramas. No actor can personate comedy unless he be a gentleman. A comedian cannot strut, cannot "take steps;" he must bear himself with the ease peculiar to perfect breeding. A dress coat is a terrible ordeal, and he who wears it triumphantly is a *rara avis*. Fechter mastered its black angles. His assumption of feigned intoxication in "On Demande un Gouverneur," was consummate. Rare is the art that can render drunkenness charming. This Fechter possessed, and at the close of the scene the impulse was to demand its repetition. It was humor devoid of grossness. Fechter could not touch anything without enveloping it in romance, and actually discovered the poetry of inebriety. He was as graceful in the vagaries of his legs as if he had been executing a *pas seul.* Fechter drunk was as versatile as Fechter sober, the real intoxication of *Don Cæsar de Bazan* being totally different in expression from that assumed by the French gentleman, *Frédéric de Marsan.*

———◆◇◆———

## "DON CÆSAR DE BAZAN."

THE text of "Don Cæsar" refers to the vagabond nobleman as "this sottish mummer," and Lemaître, the great personator of *chevaliers d'industrie,* who first produced the drama, was wont to make *Don Cæsar* very drunk ; while the elder Wallack, the original of the English version, — " the most effective personator of the hero, if not the most agreeable," says the London *Athenæum,* — descended to the vulgarity of hiccoughing. Assuredly there is no authority for this license. *Don Cæsar* has lost none of his wits, he is capable of fighting skilfully enough to kill a captain. Wine has made him familiar, affectionately demonstrative, somewhat doubtful as to his centre of gravity, and that is all. Fechter went no further, and was so delicately unctuous in this bibulous mood as to cause regret upon his returning to a normal condition. Nothing could be neater in its humor than Fechter's pantomime when, in referring to his creditors and remarking, " Most of them have children, creditors *will* have children, heirs to their ledgers," he indicated by the airiest motion *stairs* of children ascending from earth to heaven. Equally good was the broader humor of his funniest point when wrestling with a word of five syllables. " How human nature has de-gen-er — "

" Rated," added *Don José*, coming to the rescue.

" Thank you," replied *Don Cæsar*, shaking him tenderly by the hand, with inexpressible drollery, " it 's a long word." Like all his other points, it was original.

Throughout the first two acts Fechter was champagne in human form. The grace of his audacity supplied the place of virtue, and the " good fellow " was so good that reformation became a foregone conclusion. A notable feature in Fechter's acting was the artistic employment of the baldest stage accessories. When he sat down the chair became vitalized, and immediately played an effective and thoroughly appropriate part. Thus, upon *Don José's* intimating that *Don Cæsar* would die on the gallows, the noble vagabond started up, and, seizing the chair while exclaiming, " But a rope like a thief ! " raised it aloft as if to hurl it at the power which could so insult him. Though only a wooden chair, there was dignity and passion in the pose, and the action entirely harmonized with the hidalgo's hot blood. Fechter's *Don Cæsar* treated wine as if it really had wooed and won him. As he inhaled its aroma the cup seemed to brim with the true descendant of the vine, and when he next spoke his voice was flavored with it !

During the drinking chorus, it was Fechter's easy
pantomime, not the singing, that interested, and when
in the midst of the revelry the clock struck half-past
six, Fechter made a neat point by putting his finger in
his ear, as if to shut out destiny. Are these things
trivial? Not so trivial but they constitute the difference between letter and spirit. In the interviews between the *Marchioness of Santa Cruz* and *Don Cæsar*,
Fechter's gesticulation and facial expression added rich
sauce to the admirable situation, while the scene between *Don Cæsar* and the *King*, in the last act, was
rendered inimitable by Fechter's manner. " If you
are Don Cæsar de Bazan, *I* am the King of Spain ! "
Placing his hat on his head at an angle of audacious
coolness, Fechter took the stage, and, fanning himself with his pocket handkerchief, swaggered to the
foot-lights with an indescribable mock-heroic air that
inspired several rounds of applause. Authority declares that both Lemaître and the elder Wallack made
their point here by sitting opposite the *King*, and
touching the spring of a spiral feather in their hats,
which gradually rose and nodded familiarly to astounded royalty. Such loud burlesque is unwarrantable, and Fechter showed wisdom in not overstep-
ping the line of comedy. The closing scenes of the
acting within the acting were masterly strokes, as
indicative of the artist as Giotto's drawing of the
circle.

## "THE CORSICAN BROTHERS."

FAR less worthy of Fechter was the drama of "The Corsican Brothers;" not because it is melodramatic for, saving the apparitions, there is nothing that does not hold the mirror up to Corsican nature (and in these days of Spiritualism who shall say that apparitions are impossible?) but because there is hardly sufficient body to the drama. Fechter's *Fabien* and *Louis dei Franchi* were distinct and complete personations; but, remembering *Hamlet*, they were the condescensions of a king. That the general public preferred Dumas to Shakespeare was pitiable for artist and critic. Despite all cavilling, however, Fechter's face never spoke more telling, significant language than during two moments of "The Corsican Brothers," — the first when he repelled the audacity of *Celestine*, with such a look of withering contempt as would blanch the cheek of the most degraded of women; the second when, stepping between *Émilie de Lesparre* and *Chateau Renaud*, upon being appealed to by the former for protection, he completely cowed the braggart by a language of the eye that defies description and completely does away with the necessity of speech. Nothing could have been more quiet, more gentlemanly, and yet more telling. Applause followed instantaneously, even from "the gods," proving that in the good time coming the popular taste may relish something better than ranting. Fechter's Corsican dress for *Fabien* was a study, perfect in every appointment — even to the ear-rings and the tobacco-pouch from which he manufactured cigarettes as he sat on the table and related the peculiarities of his family. Those who watched narrowly remarked that as *Louis*, Fechter wore no cravat, but fastened his collar with a gold stud. Strange, for a Parisian who was so perfectly dressed in other respects. Then it was remembered that in Corsica, and even in Southern France, cravats are ignored !

A picture of the times stood on the stage ; and, in the hand-to-hand conflict that closes the drama, the audience beheld a hot-blooded Corsican tiger thirsting for revenge, fighting with all the skill and litheness of a creature brought up among mountains and *vendette*. For the first time too, in America, " The Corsican Brothers " was played as originally written. Prior to Fechter's advent the second act had been made the first, owing to a mistake of the English publisher, who accidentally reversed the order of the acts, in which order Charles Kean introduced the drama to the London public.

---

## " MONTE CRISTO."

When Fechter first appeared in his dramatization of Dumas's famous novel, many variations were heard on the well-worn theme of the sensational drama. Is not a vast deal of nonsense written and talked thereon ? It would be supposed, from the manner in which Shakespeare is lauded and melodrama derided, that the Swan of Avon swam in the most placid of mill-streams, whereas there never lived a dramatist who showed so great a mastery of effects. There is not a play of his, holding the stage, that is not in the truest sense sensational; and Shakespeare is acted, not because of his poetry, but because of his knowledge of situations and how to command the interest of an audience. " Hamlet " is full of sensation. Murder most foul and unnatural precedes it, a ghost stalks abroad in the first act, there is murder again in the third act, a mad scene and drowning in the fourth, unlimited poisoning and stabbing in the fifth act. What more sensational than *Othello's* smothering of *Desdemona ?* What more thoroughly melodramatic than the tragedy of "Macbeth?" What more opposed to nature than " Midsummer Night's Dream " and the " Tempest?" And are " Richard III." and " King Lear " pastoral poems? When Shakespeare forgets his effects he becomes a poet merely, and his plays, like those of Ben Jonson and others, are read, not acted. The theatre demands situations first, language second. The difference between Shakespeare and the highest order of sensational dramatist is that one has great genius and the other great cleverness. One is a poet as well as a playwright, and the other is merely a playwright. One ennobles his plot by the beauty of his verse ; the other belittles it by the vulgarity of his dialogue. One endows his meanest characters with intellect far beyond what each type possesses in real life ; the other gives even his heroes nothing but " situations." The greater includes the less, but the less does not include the greater. If, then, Shakespeare be good authority, melodrama is thoroughly legitimate. The sensational actor is he who produces a sensation. An audience cannot be excited without being thrilled. It cannot be thrilled without being made to feel. An actor cannot make others feel without feeling himself. He cannot feel without possessing what is called genius. It is quite possible to be a good melodramatic actor and not be able to properly interpret Shakespeare ; but the actor who takes a modern melodrama and, lifting it out of its absurdity, raises it to an ideal height, stands as an actor very near where Shakespeare stands as a dramatist. If an actor makes the impossible appear real, he has the imagination of a poet and gives evidence of greater ability than if he were personating an every-day hero.

For this reason he is mistaken who fancies that anything less than greatness produced Fechter's effect in " Monte Cristo." It would be as absurd to deny Ristori's genius in *Sister Térésa*, in *Elizabeth*, and *Marie Antoinette*. " Mrs. Siddons was quite as great in *Mrs. Beverley* and *Isabella* as in *Lady Macbeth* and *Queen Katharine;* yet no one, we apprehend, will say that the poetry is equal," says captious Hazlitt, — whose criticism applies to Fechter in the melodramas of " The Duke's Motto," " Corsican Brothers," and his own version of " Monte Cristo." It requires most natural acting to create reality under the ribs of improbability. When brought out in London, Fechter's " Monte Cristo " ran for one hundred nights. It was deservedly successful, as it is the work of a clever playwright. Ignoring the popular taste for pageantry, Fechter put aside the wondrous cave of *Monte Cristo* which plays so prominent a part in the published drama, gave but passing mention to the gorgeous *Princess Haidee*, introduced comparatively few characters, told but one of the many stories that make up the romance, told this story decisively, and did not hesitate to take liberties with the original plot for the sake of dramatic effect. Thus, for example, instead of being *Villefort's* father, *Noirtier* became his half-brother ; by which change the dramatist could, without visitings of conscience, render *Villefort* doubly treacherous toward *Noirtier*. *Mercedes* did not marry *Fernand* until eighteen years after the disappearance of *Edmond Dantes*. *Albert de Morcerf* encountered *Dantes* disguised as an abbé, at a roadside inn, instead of meeting him in Rome as the *Count of Monte Cristo*. The youth's life was saved by *Dantes* in Africa, not in Rome, and all of *Dantes's* enemies came to most dramatic grief before the final moment that witnessed the triumph of long-suffering virtue in the union of *Mercedes*, *Dantes*, and their son. These were a few of the many transformations in an old friend's features. The entire first act was a condensation of Dumas's first two chapters. The drama was no worse in dialogue than the " Corsican Brothers." Occasional slips of phraseology attested its French origin, — slips so palpable as to render their retention more than strange. The plot was good, but, oddly enough, Fechter actually failed to make his own hero as all-pervading as his audiences desired.

In the first act Fechter was every inch a sailor; in the second his prison " make up " was admirable. In the third act, his disguise as an abbé was most artistic, and his acting worthy of his dress ; but it was not until the fourth act that he gave himself an opportunity for the display of his best genius. In the garb of the *Count of Monte Cristo* he was the perfection of manner and neat acting. No actor can personate high comedy unless he have the instincts of a gentleman. Fechter's interview with *Mercedes* was marked by all the intense passion for which his name was a synonyme ; and the action and facial expression with which he recognized, in *Albert de Morcerf*, his own son was so thrillingly magnetic as to be received with call upon call. The fifth act exhibited Fechter's consummate skill in fencing, and when the curtain fell it fell upon the last of a series of fine tableaux. From the beginning to the end of the drama the massing of colors and disposition of figures denoted Fechter's complete knowledge of his profession, which commanded for him the respect of all who appreciate its rarity. Draughtsman no less than author and actor, Fechter's handiwork was visible in the designs for the scenery so beautifully painted. There has seldom been seen on any stage a finer work of art than the interior and exterior of Chateau d'If, the island prison in which *Dantes* is buried alive, as presented at the Globe Theatre, Boston. The foreground disclosed the dungeons of *Dantes* and *Abbé Faria,* with ramparts above, on which a guard patroled ; in the background the chateau's gloomy tower frowned upon the cliff beneath and the threatening sky above. By sinking the dungeons the interior speedily disappeared, and then the previously brewing storm broke out. Lightning, thunder, rain, and wind were so real as to deceive the acutest eyes and ears. Fechter's devices in conjuring the elements, especially water, were those of a wizard. Angry waves dashed to and fro, and amidst this war of nature two guards, bearing the supposed dead body of *Faria*, but in theatrical reality that of the living *Dantes*, slowly ascended the steep steps leading to the summit of the cliff, where the body was hurled into the sea. Guards disappeared; the storm lulled ; *Dantes* rose to the surface of the water, climbed to the top of a rock, fell on his knees, and, extending his arms towards heaven, exclaimed with electrifying passion : " Saved ! Mine the treasures of Monte Cristo ! The world is mine ! " Gustave Doré, in his best moment, could not improve this picture. Scenery without acting is a Barmecide feast. With Fechter it was an exquisite frame, setting off the painting of an artist.

# RECOLLECTIONS OF CHARLES FECHTER.

———◆———

BY

EDMUND YATES,

HERMAN VEZIN,

AND

WILKIE COLLINS.

# EXPLANATORY NOTE.

——◆——

EVER since I have had ears to hear I have been told that, wonderful as women may be in instinct, they are totally without reason. Being creatures of emotion, loving or hating from impulse, they lack the judicial element, and consequently are incapable of genuine criticism. I am a woman, and what I have written of Fechter the Artist is doomed to be attributed, by some at least, to the fervid fancy of a female partisan ; though I am no partisan, though Fechter and I were strangers in his closing years. It is a coincidence that the words, "Remember me," written for me by Fechter, on a beautiful crayon head of himself as *Hamlet*, should have faded out of sight about the time that the giver proved unkind.

He is base indeed who allows his estimate of an artist to be warped by personal feelings. Fechter was no less great in his art when he turned his back on his friends ; and my enthusiasm is as warm to-day as when he first revealed himself. No one has taken his place. In vain have I sought to find his peer at the Comédie Française and elsewhere in Paris. No Fechter has arisen, and the Romantic Drama languishes. "I'd almost be willing to be twenty years older for the sake of having seen him in his prime, when he played *Armand Duval* with Madame Doche," ex-claims a woman and a critic. What greater sacrifice than this could a woman make to art? To add twenty years to her age! "The last time I saw Fechter," continues this critic, "was in Philadelphia, one year before he died. I was standing in front of the Conti-nental Hotel as he went down Ninth Street, wearing a long frock coat buttoned to the chin, and a low-crowned broad-brimmed beaver hat. I don't know which he the more resembled, priest or planter, but there was a distinction about him that was impressive, and it did not seem right to let him pass by without some sort of demonstration."

Because I am a woman, — because I know how many enemies Fechter the Man made in this country, and how few are willing in consequence to do him justice, — I have appealed to critics in England to place them-selves on record for art's sake. No better judges of acting live than the three men who generously respond. As good wine needs no bush, the names of Wilkie Col-lins and Edmund Yates need no introduction. It is our misfortune though not our fault that, American though he be, Herman Vezin should have won his laurels upon the English stage, and only be known to his travelled countrymen. Standing in the front rank of his profession, Herman Vezin is a rare example of culture and probity. Of such stuff should all actors be made.

KATE FIELD.

# EDMUND YATES ON CHARLES FECHTER.

———◆———

THE first time I ever saw Fechter on the stage was in the spring of 1852, when I was a young man of twenty, highly impressionable, and devoted to the drama. He played *Armand* in the " Dame aux Camélias," with Madame Doche as heroine. I thought it then a most striking performance, and it still remains so in my memory. *Armand* is what actors call merely a " feeder " to *Marguerite*, — save in one act, when he turns upon her ; and there Fechter, in his alternating rage, love, and despair, was almost sublime. I made his personal acquaintance when he first came to England, about the year 1859 or 1860, and as I was then living in his immediate neighborhood, in St. John's Wood, we were thrown much together, and became very intimate.

Another neighbor and prominent member of our circle was the Rev. J. N. Bellew, at that time incumbent of St. Mark's, Hamilton Terrace, an enthusiastic Shakespearian, to whom unquestionably Fechter was greatly indebted for much of the best of his conception of *Hamlet*. At the time I speak of, and for several years afterwards, Fechter was the most abstemious of

men ; he ate sparingly, and never drank anything but a
little claret and water. He was most domestic in his
habits, and devoted to his two children, — especially to
his son, little Paul. His health was not good ; he had
some extraordinary complaint which no one could ever
get at, but which had the effect of causing a sudden
swelling — as he described it, " a gonflement " — of the
stomach, which caused him much pain and frequently
incapacitated him from acting.

At such times he would go to bed and lie there
moaning dismally, with his head tied up in a handkerchief, with a cataplasm on his stomach, tisane to drink,
and all those weak and washy solaces and medicaments
with which a sick Frenchman loves to surround himself.

He was the best love-maker I ever saw on the stage ;
he threw his whole heart and soul into it, and made
love not merely in words but with the inflections of
his voice, with his attitudes, with his eyes. *Ruy Blas*
was unquestionably his best part. It had no blot.
His love for the *Queen* was most charmingly expressed ;
and in the last act of rage and vengeance on the trai-
tor he was positively sublime. Mounet-Sully, who is
the present *Ruy Blas* of the Comédie Française, and
who appeared in England with Sara Bernhardt, is not
to be compared to Fechter. I am afraid Lewes is right
about his *Othello*. It was a desperately poor performance, full of French tricks and nonsense ; but, on the
other hand, his *Iago* was admirable. " Hamlet " was
the play with which he made most money. He had
extraordinary dramatic power off the stage. Many
and many a time he has kept me up till two or three in

the morning, telling the plot of some piece which he intended to produce, and walking about the room, acting each scene and each character. He had a most unhappy knack of quarrelling with people, — often those with whom he had been most intimate.

I recollect Dickens saying to me of him once that he had never met anybody with greater appreciative power of reading character. " He seemed," Dickens said, " to combine a man's insight with a woman's instinct."

EDMUND YATES.

# HERMAN VEZIN ON CHARLES FECHTER.

———◆———

FECHTER made an immediate and decided hit. There was a vivacity, a charm, a grace and fervor in his acting which — impregnated as it was with his French manner — struck us all as so fresh and original that he became the talk of London. Harris, the manager, had taken care to have him surrounded with the best procurable talent, and the new scenery and dresses for "Ruy Blas" — Falconer's translation — were most complete in design and rich in material. Nothing was left undone that could aid his success. Fechter himself had passed some time in London prior to his appearance, making many friends and exciting curiosity amongst those whose opinion would be of value to him.

I was introduced to Fechter soon after his appearance. His manner of clinging to one's hand and looking with his beautiful eyes into one's own, as if this moment was the one he had lived for, was very fetching ; and charming he undoubtedly was until you quarrelled with him, and then —

"Ruy Blas" was succeeded by "Don Cæsar de Bazan," "The Golden Dagger," etc., none of which plays did more than confirm Fechter's fame. At last he played *Hamlet*, and took the town by storm. His appearance, his easy grace, his freedom from the vice of mouthing, his unstilted style, delighted all but the most bigoted adherents of the stagey school of acting. I sat in the stalls at one of the rehearsals, and was much struck by his manner of always thinking the thought of *Hamlet* before he spoke the words. I said to him, " You are going to make a great hit in this part." Years afterwards he recalled my words, and added, " You were the only one who encouraged me." It was amusing to observe the absurd forms the enthusiasm he excited sometimes took. I watched two women one night, panting and gasping with ecstasy ; and, as Fechter left the stage, one of them exclaimed, " Why, he even speaks English better than an English actor !" A critic of some prominence remarked very sagely, " Why should Mr. Fechter be reproached for acting *Hamlet* with a foreign accent? for, after all, *Hamlet* was not an Englishman." " Hamlet " had a run, unprecedented at that time, of seventy-five nights. Soon after this, Fechter took the Lyceum Theatre.

Whether he was backed by a wealthy admirer or not, I don't know ; but he went to work as if he had been possessed of a Fortunatus purse. He engaged Phelps, Mr. and Mrs. Charles Mathews, and Walter Montgomery, — none of whom ever appeared at his theatre. His first production, " The Duke's Motto," which he had expected to run a few weeks only, ran a whole season, to immense business. He then reconstructed his stage and machinery, importing a posse of French carpenters to show the Englishmen how to work the machinery. One of them, after putting a piece of scenery into its proper place, turned to his English brother and said, "Comme ça!" The next night the English carpenter did the work, the Frenchman looking on to supervise. The English brother above alluded to, on repeating the work of the Frenchman, looked up at the piece of scenery he had just handled, and muttered: "Comme ça! You can't get on with this —— scenery unless you speak French to it!"

Nothing could exceed the exquisite beauty and skill of Fechter's stage management. I played with him in "The Master of Ravenswood," "Hamlet," and "The Corsican Brothers," and I found him perfectly unselfish and an artist "aux bouts des ongles." He never thought of depending entirely upon himself. He engaged the best actors he could get, and spared no expense in scenery and appointments. He never sacrificed another actor to himself on the stage. Every one had his chance, and he must have been a dullard who did not profit by his invaluable hints.

Fechter was essentially a great expert. His art presented no difficulties he could not surmount. It must be confessed, however, that when an author's creation was beyond his grasp, he dragged the author down to his own level, as was the case in *Othello*, the greatest of parts; but even in this failure he did things which were exquisite in their grace and finish.

As Dickens said, Fechter had a genius for quarrelling, and no doubt his ungovernable temper was the primary cause of his downfall. Any opposition seemed to make him mad, and in these fits he would ruthlessly insult his best friends so grossly as to make all reconciliation impossible, even if he had sought it ; but this he never did. It was a wonder that he never quarrelled with Dickens.

His character was not without reproach ; but he has left his mark on the stage, and all actors who had the intelligence to appreciate him, owe him an artistic debt. His *Iago* was much liked and was highly artistic, but none of his Shakespearian attempts equalled his *Hamlet*. Hermann Hendrich was, in my opinion, the very finest *Hamlet* I have ever seen. Still, Fechter will rank high in the roll of great actors who have excelled in that character.

HERMAN VEZIN.

# WILKIE COLLINS'S RECOLLECTIONS OF CHARLES FECHTER.

———◆———

I FIRST saw Fechter in Paris nearly thirty years since, on the stage of the old Vaudeville Theatre. He had then lately achieved one of the great triumphs of his art, by playing the part of *Armand Duval* in the first, and (speaking in a dramatic sense) the best of the plays of Alexander Dumas the younger, — "La Dame aux Camélias."

When he came to London, in 1860, to act, for the first time in the English language, in a translation of "Ruy Blas," we were made personally known to one another.

By common impulse we dispensed with the tentative formalities of acquaintance, and became friends from that day to the day of Fechter's death.

I have been asked to write my recollections of this admirable actor and delightful companion. It is useless to conceal that this is a melancholy task. I must look back at some of those happiest days of my life, which are days that I can never see again ; and I must write composedly and impartially — if I can — of a friend who held a place in my regard which has never since been filled.

Such remembrances as I can offer to readers with propriety divide themselves, to my mind, into two parts. Permit me to call them FECHTER IN PUBLIC and FECHTER IN PRIVATE.

## FECHTER IN PUBLIC.

It has been said, most truly, that the art of the actor dies with him.

No description of acting, by a person who has seen the player, can convey any distinct idea to the mind of a person who has not seen the player. For example, it has not been our good fortune to go to the theatre in the time of the great Garrick. What do we know of his acting, from the many careful and conscientious descriptions of it which have appeared in print? We know absolutely nothing but the result. In tragedy and comedy alike, Garrick delighted everybody who was fortunate enough to see him.

To take another example, — Macready, in his youth, had the honor of acting with Mrs. Siddons. He played *Norval* to her *Lady Randolph* in the tragedy of "Douglas."

I once asked him if he could tell me anything which would give me some idea of her acting. He answered : " I can only tell you this ; in the scene in which she recognizes *Norval* as her lost son she gave me a hug that hurt me, and I felt her tears dropping on my face." Let it not be forgotten that she must, at this late date in her career, have played *Lady Randolph* during the theatrical engagements of many years, — and we derive from such testimony as this the vague idea of a grand passionate actress, so absolutely identified with her part that no frequency of repetition could weaken or degrade her performance. But do we advance a step farther? Do we hear the tones which gave a charm, not its own, to the prosy poetry of the play?

Do we see the beautiful face expressing the pathetic exultation of maternal love? Can we, in the remotest degree, feel what the audience must have felt when her tears dropped on Macready's face? We know no more about it than that much injured man, the ex-king of the Zulus.

For these good reasons I shall not waste words in any attempt to revive the dead and buried influences of Fechter's acting by describing it in detail. Those unfortunate people who have not seen him must remain in their darkness. Nothing can now enlighten them.

Speaking of his acting in general terms only, I may say that it was noble and romantic,—with this inestimable merit added, that it was always firmly founded on truth to nature. His style was, to use the painter's phrase, broad.

In his least successful efforts he always avoided that excessive accumulation of detail which still deteriorates so much good acting in these later days. In the all-important accomplishment of "making love" on the stage he was rivalled by but one man, in my dramatic experience, — and that man was always helped by music, — the irresistible Mario.

Fechter's knowledge of his art, and his eye for dramatic effect, made him invaluable at rehearsal.

He was an excellent adviser when a new play was in course of production, — to the writer as well as to the performers. There are living actors and actresses who can still bear witness, on the stage, to an advance in their art due to his teaching and example, which has worthily raised them in the estimation of the public. The Miss Kate Terry (of those days), Miss Carlotta Leclercq (still on the stage), were, as actresses, almost created anew by their dramatic association with Fechter. No foreigner ever grappled more resolutely and successfully than he did with the difficulties of the English language. He told me that to speak with ease and propriety the one line in *Hamlet's* soliloquy, "What's Hecuba to him, or he to Hecuba?" was a labor of weeks. Allowing all due force to the influence of such determined application as this, the secret of his instantaneous success, when he first stepped on our stage in the character of an English actor, lay really and truly in his consummate knowledge of his art.

Long before we, in front of the curtain, had discovered what he could do in *Ruy Blas* as an actor, we had only to observe his movements, his manner, his by-play, to be free from the slightest apprehension of his breaking down under the hard stress of speaking to us in our language.

As to the relative value of Fechter's performances in England, I believe I only express the general opinion when I place *Ruy Blas* and *Hamlet* in the front rank.

With regard to Victor Hugo's powerful play, I do not hesitate to say (speaking from an experience which, be it remembered, does not include Edmund Kean) that

Fechter's *Ruy Blas* was the nearest approach to perfection, as a performance in romantic drama, that we have seen in England in later years, — reserving the one exception of the one supremely great actor, Frédéric Lemaître. Speaking next of *Hamlet*, I will only venture to give my evidence as a witness. From Macready downward I have, I think, seen every *Hamlet* of any note and mark during the last five and thirty years. The true *Hamlet* I first saw when Fechter stepped on the stage. These words, if they merely expressed my own opinion, it is needless to say would never have been written. But they express the opinion of every unprejudiced person, under fifty years of age, with whom I have met. For that reason, let the words stand.

In the long list of his performances of the second order — or, to speak more exactly, in characters of secondary importance from the theatrical point of view — I may specify *Monte Cristo*, *Edgar* in an adaptation of the immortal "Bride of Lammermoor," *Claude Melnotte* in the "Lady of Lyons," the double characters in "The Duke's Motto" (names forgotten), *Obenreizer* in "No Thoroughfare," and *Maurice de Layrac* in "Black and White."

Approaching once more the throne of Shakespeare, I should add that I have heard almost universal praise of Fechter's *Iago*, — which I did not see, — and that I have nothing to say of his *Othello* except to express my regret that I *did* see it. The sooner that unfortunate performance is buried in oblivion, the better.

All that I can usefully write of my friend in his public capacity has now come to an end. Having already described him as a master of his art, I have implied that he set the mark of invention and fancy of a high order on his management of the stage. Costume and scenery, color and grouping, theatrical effect as assisted by paints, powders, and wigs, — all felt his influence for good. These attendant merits deserve to be specially mentioned. They rank among the minor means which helped him to his brilliant success in England. The drawbacks to that success behind the scenes — the mortification that he suffered from the jealousy and ingratitude of some of his professional brethren — I purposely pass over. No foul tongues can reach him now. The consecration of Death holds him sacred from insult.

### FECHTER IN PRIVATE.

One of the worst vices of the age we live in is the shameless disregard of truth prevalent among friends, writing or speaking in public, of celebrated persons whom they have survived. Unblushing exaggeration of the merits, position, and influence of the dead man seems to be considered as sufficient warrant for a deliberate concealment of his failings and faults, — which is nothing less than lying of the passive sort, artfully adapted to its purpose as a pedestal on which the writer or speaker can present himself to the public in a favorable light. Persons in general wishing, in the case of a famous man deceased, to find out what sort of man he really was, are in these days invited to look at a fancy portrait (greasy with the varnish of fulsome praise) in place of a true likeness ; and, worse still, are pestered by the appearance of the begging-box, sent round by public advertisement, in the interests of a posthumous glory shining with a false light.

Trifling as they may be, these recollections of Fechter shall deceive no one. They shall present the side of his character which deserves blame as faithfully as they present the side of his character which deserves praise.

Telling the truth for truth's sake, I may serve one useful purpose at least. I may perhaps relieve innocent people from reports which have cruelly and ignorantly associated them with the disasters of the closing years of my friend's life.

The serious defects of Fechter's character were two in number. The first of these his friends viewed with regret. From the second, they could only turn away in despair.

I have met with many children who had a clearer idea then he possessed of pecuniary responsibilities. When he wanted money he borrowed it of the first friend whom he met, with the firmest imaginary belief in his capacity to make repayment at the shortest possible date. Under the same delusion he allowed greedy adventurers, in want of supplies, to involve him in debt with tradespeople by making their purchases in his name. His sympathy with worthier friends in a state of pecuniary embarrassment was boundless. When he had no money to spare, and he was asked for a loan of " a few hundred pounds," he had no hesitation in borrowing the money from the friend who had it, and handing the sum over to the friend who had it not.

When I remonstrated with him, he was always ready with his answer. " My dear Wilkie, you know I love you. Do you think I should love you if I did n't firmly believe that you would do just the same thing in my place?" He might have ended, poor fellow, by putting me in the wrong in a better way than this; he might have paid all his debts, and died with a mind at ease, but for that second defect in his character, to which it is now my hard duty to allude.

The curse of an ungovernable temper was the curse of Fechter's life.

I am not speaking of mere outbreaks of furious anger. He was too sensitive and too generous a man not to be able to atone for forgetting himself in this way, as soon as his composure was restored. But, when he once took offence, a lurking devil saturated his whole being with the poison of unjust suspicion and inveterate hatred ; and that devil, the better influences about him, distrusted rather than encouraged by himself, were powerless to cast out.

I have no heart to dwell on the number of friends (honestly admiring him, eager to serve him, guiltless of consciously offending him) whom he estranged forever, — self-deceived by his own impulsive misinterpretation of motives, or misled by false reports which he had no patience to examine before he accepted them as truths. When he first fascinated American audiences (there is no exaggeration of his influence in using that word) he was offered, by formal agreement, pecuniary prospects which would have assured to him, as the reward for a few years' exercise of his art, a more than sufficient income for life. He quarrelled with the man, the thoroughly honest and responsible man, who made him that offer. At a little social gathering, in the United States, the friend thus estranged said to me, "To this day, I don't know what I did to give offence."

Other persons present were surprised to see that he spoke with tears in his eyes. I, who knew the irresistible attraction of Fechter, when he was in possession of himself, understood and respected that honest distress. It is useless to pursue this subject by citing other examples. When Fechter died in poverty, far away from relatives and friends in the Old World, it is not true — I assert it from what I myself had opportunities of knowing — it is not true to say that the miserable end was due to connections which he formed in the United States. The one enemy to his prosperity was the enemy in himself. He paid the penalty of his ungovernable temper, — and no man can own it with truer sorrow than the man who has reluctantly written these lines.

Let us pass into a brighter atmosphere. Before we leave him, let us see him at his best.

The sensitive nature of the man — undoubtedly the motive-power of the all-attractive social influence by which his friends delight to remember him — showed itself noticeable in what I may call the private practice of his art. He will be, perhaps, most intelligibly revealed in this aspect, if I consult my own experience of him at a time when we were engaged together in preparing a play for the stage.

I had the honor of writing the Christmas story called " No Thoroughfare " in literary association with Charles Dickens. We invented the story at Gadshill, in the Swiss châlet which had been Fechter's gift to Dickens. When our last page of manuscript had been set up in type, I returned to other literary labors which had been suspended in favor of " No Thoroughfare," and which kept me so closely employed that I saw nothing of my brethren in art for some little time. During this interval Fechter had read the proof-sheets, had (to use his own phrase) " fallen madly in love with the subject," and had prepared a *scenario* or outline of a dramatic adaptation of the story, under Dickens's superintendence and approval. This done, Dickens took his departure for the United States, leaving the destinies of the unwritten play safe, as he kindly said, in my hands. Fechter next presented himself with the *scenario*, laid the manuscript on my desk, offered me a pen with a low bow, and said : " Dickens has gone away for six months ; he will find ' No Thoroughfare ' running when he comes back." For once, in this case, a modern prophecy was actually fulfilled.

The play written, — a far harder task than I had anticipated, requiring such new presentation of some of the persons of the story as almost involved the re-creating of them, — Fechter at once assumed the character of *Obenreizer* in private life. When he entered his study or mine, it was an entrance on the stage. He ate and drank " in character " when he dined with me or I dined with him. The play was in his hands all day and at his bedside all night. At rehearsal he was quite ready to perform every other character in the drama, by way of an example which might brighten and improve the business on the stage. Once or twice the overwhelming nervous excitement that possessed him showed itself in a curiously suggestive way; his English speech betrayed, for the first time in my experience, that he was thinking in French.

When the memorable day arrived, and a few hours only interposed between us and the ordeal of the first night, that terrible form of nervous prostration called stage fright — from which all good actors suffer, more or less, at their first appearance in a new part — began its attack on Fechter at breakfast time.

He could eat nothing, not even the French garlic sausage which offered the one attainable refuge to his stomach on other occasions. Pale, silent, subdued, he sat in a corner of the room, and looked like a man waiting the appearance of the sheriff to conduct him to the scaffold. I handed him his pipe; he was not even able to smoke. "Are you going in front to see your play?" he asked, with a look of blank despair. I could honestly answer that my nerves were never strong enough to endure that trial on the first night. "You will be behind the scenes, then?" "Yes." "For God's sake, come to my room!"

Before the performance began, I went accordingly to Fechter's room.

Dressed, as to the lower part of him only, for the character of *Obenreizer*, he sat helplessly staring into a white basin, held before him by his attendant in the attitude of a sailor on a channel steamer comforting a

suffering lady. " Here 's Mr. Fechter sick, sir," said
the man, " and nothing in him to bring up." (The
reader will, I hope, pardon this literal report in consideration of its absolute fidelity to the truth.) I said
a comforting word, and proposed a few drops of lau-
danum. Unable to speak, Fechter answered by putting out his tongue. The color of it had turned, under
the nervous terror that possessed him, to the metallic
blackness of the tongue of a parrot. When the over-
ture began, — easily audible in the dressing-room, —
another attack made the basin necessary.

In the interval that followed, *Obenreizer's* upper garments were put on, and the last touches were added to
his head and face. The next sound that reached us
was the well deserved applause which greeted the appearance of that admirable actor and worthy kind-
hearted man, Benjamin Webster, in the character of
*Joey Ladle.* Fechter gave me one expressive look,
and turned to the basin again. His colleague's entrance on the stage preceded his own entrance by no
very long space of time. Soon the knock was heard at
the door, and the dreadful voice of the call-boy sum-
moned Mr. Fechter to be ready. He took my arm
to descend the stairs which led from his room to the
stage. Our procession of two was completed by the
attendant with his basin ready, — and, what is more,
wanted, at the critical moment when we stood behind
the door through which *Obenreizer* was to make his
appearance. Some one near me whispered, " Good
heavens, he will be taken ill before the audience ! " I
whispered back, " Wait and see." In another minute
the words were spoken which gave him the cue.

"Ask Mr. Obenreizer to step this way." The door was briskly opened ; the glare of the footlights shone on the favorite of the public ; the round of applause at the sight of him rang out all over the crowded theatre. In an instant the moral courage, which had deserted him behind the scenes, rallied its forces in the presence of the audience. Fechter's first words proved him to be in full possession of all his resources. The stranger who had predicted such terrible results lifted his eyebrows in mute amazement. The attendant and the basin vanished together.

" No Thoroughfare " had a run of two hundred nights. We were not so fortunate in making our next joint appeal to the public, in the drama called " Black and White."

Fechter's lively mind was, to use his own expression, "full of plots." He undertook to tell me stories enough for all the future novels and plays that I could possibly live to write. His power of invention was unquestionably remarkable ; but his method of narration was so confused that it was not easy to follow him, and his respect for those terrible obstacles in the way of free imagination known as probabilities was, to say the least of it, in some need of improvement.

One of his plots, however, he presented intelligibly in the form of a *scenario.* The story, as I thought and still think, was full of dramatic interest. Following Fechter's outline in the first two acts, and suggesting a new method of concluding the story, to which he agreed, I wrote the drama called " Black and White," being solely responsible for the conception and development of the characters, and for the dialogue attributed to them.

This work, presented for the first time to the public
at the Adelphi Theatre, London, on the 29th of March,
1869, was received by the audience of the first night
with tumultuous applause, Fechter's performance of
the principal part being even finer than his performance of *Obenreizer.*

As a play, "Black and White" was considered by
my literary brethren (and justly considered) to be
better work than "No Thoroughfare." We left the
theatre with the fairest prospect of another run of
six months. But, after some few weeks the regular
Adelphi audience reminded us gently, by means of
vacant places in the theatre, of an objection to the
play which had never once occurred to either of us.
We had completely forgotten the popular mania of seventeen years before, satirized by the French as *Oncle
Tommerie.* Almost every theatre in Great Britain had,
in those days, provided an adaptation of "Uncle Tom's
Cabin." It mattered nothing that the scene of "Black
and White" was laid far away from the United States,
in the Island of Trinidad, and that not one of the persons
of the drama recalled the characters in Mrs. Stowe's
novel in the slightest degree. Mrs. Stowe's subject was
slavery, and our subject was slavery; and even the long-
suffering English public had had enough of it.

*We* had had enough of it, in our different way, after
the piece had been performed about sixty nights.
What would the scene-painters, carpenters, property-
men, and supernumeraries, who now make dramas for

the theatre, assisted, it is right to add, by a handy occasional person called an author, — what would these collaborators say to a run of sixty nights? They would say : "You made a great mistake ; address the eyes, ears, and noses of the audience, and (consciously or unconsciously) you may reproduce anything that has been done before ; but if you *will* meddle with the minds of the audience, then they begin to think, and no theatrical human being can answer for the consequences."

Enough, by this time, of the stage, — even in recollections of an actor.

There is a little villa in the northwestern suburb of London, close to the eastward extremity of St. John's Wood Road, which I can never pass now without a feeling of sadness. It is the last house inhabited by Fechter during his sojourn in England. Here we feasted and laughed and revelled in some of the brightest social enjoyments that life can afford. What a dreadful barrenness stares at me from those doors and windows now !

The conventional restraints of society have a use and a value which are not to be denied. But it is equally indisputable that they exact burdensome observances from men in want of recreation after that hardest of all work, which is the work of the brain done in the service of the arts. The formal assumption of evening dress, the introductions to strangers, the effort of conversation, the necessity of listening with the same polite attention to tiresome people and agreeable people alike, — these and other social sacrifices, so easy to the idle or the lightly employed guest, exact a merciless strain on the nerves of a man whose fancy and imagination, whose utmost creative powers, have been heavily taxed for hours together. He has made himself agreeable, he has enlarged his circle of acquaintances, he has perhaps strengthened his influence among certain classes ; but he has not rested after his work, and he knows it when he rises the next morning.

After his arrival in England, Fechter's success won him his entrance into society. He was welcome everywhere, and he made himself worthy of his reception in the best sense of the word. But the time came when he felt the strain on his resources. He applied the remedy ; he folded up his dress coat; he threw away his white cravat. Thenceforth, when he had his free evenings, he offered up polite apologies on the altar of society, and enjoyed himself, as the wise populace expresses it, in his own way.

Sometimes he dined with his friends, and oftener his friends dined with him. In either case we were as independent of formalities as the monks of Theleme themselves. But one rule existed ; punctuality to the dinner-hour was insisted on. I record it with pride ; the one act of folly never committed by any one of us was the folly of waiting for a late guest.

The evenings at Fechter's house present the best picture of Fechter.

In the summer time his guests generally found him waiting for them in the front garden, in his dressing-gown and slippers. The Frenchwoman who cooked for him — one of the finest artists that ever handled a saucepan — came out to tell us when dinner was ready. Nobody (the master of the house included) had any special place at the table, but everybody sat where he might, had his own little cruet-stand, and never troubled his neighbors for the necessary condiments. No servants waited on us. The cellar was on the sideboard. Each guest picked out the wines that he liked best, and put the bottle by him when he took his chair. The dogs dined with us, and friends' dogs were welcome. People who could not speak English spoke French ; and Englishmen in the same predicament stuck to their own language, — expressive pantomime being used on either side in illustration of the meaning. Anybody who felt the heat was requested to take off his coat and dine in his shirt-sleeves. Any guest, particularly skilled in the preparation of a special dish, went into the kitchen and helped the cook. Sometimes Gassier stuffed the tomatoes and Fechter brought up the dish. We had every variety of French cookery, — and twice we put the inexhaustible resources of gastronomic France to the test by dining on one article of food only, presented under many different forms. We had a potato dinner in six courses, and an egg dinner in eight courses. Never did the perfect freedom and gayety of the talk suffer shipwreck on the perilous rocks of religion and politics. A disputatious man would not have had a chance of using his tongue at that table.

The gushes of merriment were as inexhaustible as the gushes of garlic. The smoking began, as the smoking always should begin, the moment dinner was

over. With the appearance of the coffee, the amuse-
ments of the evening took a new turn. Guests possessed of special accomplishments now assumed a
prominent place. Friendly singers and musicians, well
known to the public, showed us what their art could
do. Fechter's never flagging gayety exhibited him in
a new character, — as a low comedian and a mimic.
He played, for instance, a little French scene — in which
the persons were a thief under examination, and a *juge
d'instruction* completely baffled by the dense stupidity
of the prisoner — with a perfection of quaint humor not
to be forgotten and not to be described. Equally irresistible were his imitations of the elder Dumas writing
one of his magnificent novels in a race against time,
and of another far less illustrious literary man trying to
shave himself in a state of intoxication. Equal to
Fechter in fertility of resource, the kind-hearted, genial
Gassier was ready to sing any operatic music within the
reach of his fine baritone voice, and was so skilled a
musician that he invented his own accompaniment on
the piano when memory and music-books happened to
fail him.

In the intervals of these special entertainments,
actors deservedly eminent on the French stage interested us by talk of their art, and by remembrances of
their famous colleagues. That accomplished and ele-
gant comedian, Berton the elder, told us how they
worked at the rehearsals of " The Demi-monde." Maurice Desrieux — the most lovable and most affectionate of men, the wise, patient, and devoted friend of
Fechter — described the strain laid on his dramatic

resources by the dangerous situations in the fourth act of Sardou's " Maison Neuve," in which the main responsibility rested on the character which he played in the piece. Of these three variously gifted men, — Gassier, Berton, Desrieux, — not one survives. Shall I write of other guests, and perhaps recall more pleasant voices that are now silent forever? Once more the shadow of Death darkens my view of the past. It is time to have done.

When I visited the United States in the years 1873–4, Fechter's was the first face I saw on disembarking at the wharf. We went together to my hotel in New York, and he gave me the benefit of his experience in ordering my first American dinner. He left me at night with a parting flash of the old gayety. " You will find friends here, wherever you go," he said ; " Don't forget that I was the friend who introduced you to Soft Shell Crab."

But there was a change — a melancholy change — in him, which I soon discovered. Although he shrank from confessing it, signs not to be mistaken told me that he was brooding over his wasted opportunities and his doubtful future. The happiest days of his life were now passed at his little farm in Pennsylvania. There I visited him, sincerely regretting that public engagements limited me to a sojourn of a few days only. In my travels afterwards, whenever we could meet we did meet. When I left New York for the last time, he dined with me. The two or three other friends who were of the party remarked the depression of his spirits. We parted, — not to meet again.

I wish I could add to these last words some of the letters addressed to me by Fechter, which I have thought it right to preserve. Even these are not only too personal to be presented to the public, but they are, in many places, so expressed (unconsciously on his part, it is needless to say) as to be in danger of leading to erroneous impressions of him in the minds of strangers.

This memorial portrait of Fechter would not be improved as a likeness by borrowing his own words.

Writing to me on the death of a friend whom we both dearly loved, Charles Dickens says, " We must close the ranks and march on." On a dreary English winter day I close these pages, and escape from my recollections by turning to my work.

WILKIE COLLINS.

London, 18th January, 1882.

# PRESS  NOTICES

# FECHTER'S  ACTING.

# PRESS NOTICES ON FECHTER'S ACTING.

———◆———

THE distinguished artist, whose name is prefixed to these remarks, purposes to leave England for a professional tour in the United States. A few words from me, in reference to his merits as an actor, I hope may not be uninteresting to some readers, in advance of his publicly proving them before an American audience, and I know will not be unacceptable to my intimate friend. I state at once that Mr. Fechter holds that relation towards me; not only because it is the fact, but also because our friendship originated in my public appreciation of him. I had studied his acting closely, and had admired it highly, both in Paris and in London, years before we exchanged a word. Consequently, my appreciation is not the result of personal regard, but personal regard has sprung out of my appreciation.

The first quality observable in Mr. Fechter's acting is, that it is in the highest degree romantic. However elaborated in minute details, there is always a peculiar dash and vigor in it, like the fresh atmosphere of the story whereof it is a part. When he is on the stage, it seems to me as though the story were transpiring before me for the first and last time. Thus there is a fervor in his love-making — a suffusion of his whole being with the rapture of his passion — that sheds a glory on its object, and raises her, before the eyes of the audience, into the light in which he sees her.

It was this remarkable power that took Paris by storm, when he became famous in the lover's part in the " Dame aux Camélias." It is a short part, really comprised in two scenes; but, as he acted it (he was its original representative), he left its poetic and exalting influence on the heroine throughout the play. A woman who could be so beloved, who could be so devotedly and romantically adored, had a hold upon the general sympathy with which nothing less absorbing and complete could have invested her.

When I first saw this play and this actor, I could not, in forming my lenient judgment of the heroine, forget that she had been the inspiration of a passion of which I had beheld such profound and affecting marks. I said to myself, as a child might have said: " A bad woman could not have been the object of that wonderful tenderness, could not have subdued that worshipping heart, could not have drawn such tears from such a lover." I am persuaded that the same effect was wrought upon the Parisian audiences, both consciously and unconsciously, to a very great extent, and that what was morally disagreeable in the " Dame aux Camélias " first got lost in this brilliant halo of romance. I have seen the same play with the same part otherwise acted, and in exact degree as the love became dull and earthy, the heroine descended from her pedestal.

In " Ruy Blas," in " The Master of Ravenswood,"

and in " The Lady of Lyons," — three dramas in which
Mr. Fechter especially shines as a lover, — but notably
in the first, this remarkable power of surrounding the
beloved creature, in the eyes of the audience, with the
fascination that she has for him, is strikingly displayed.
That observer must be cool indeed who does not feel,
when *Ruy Blas* stands in the presence of the young
unwedded *Queen of Spain*, that the air is enchanted;
or when she bends over him, leaving her tender touch
upon his bloody breast, that it is better so to die than
to live apart from her, and that she is worthy to be so
died for. When the *Master of Ravenswood* declares
his love for *Lucy Ashton*, and she hers for him, and
when, in a burst of rapture, he kisses the skirt of her
dress, we feel as though we touched it with our lips
to stay our goddess from soaring away into the very
heavens. And when they plight their troth and break
the piece of gold, it is we — not *Edgar* — who quickly
exchange our half for the half she was about to hang
around her neck, solely because the latter has for an instant touched the bosom we so dearly love. Again, in
" The Lady of Lyons," the picture on the easel in the
poor cottage studio is not the unfinished portrait of a
vain and arrogant girl, but becomes the sketch of a
soul's high ambition and aspiration here and hereafter.

Picturesqueness is a quality above all others pervading Mr. Fechter's assumptions. Himself a skilled
painter and sculptor, learned in the history of costume,
and informing those accomplishments and that knowledge with a similar infusion of romance (for romance
is inseparable from the man), he is always a picture, —

always a picture in its right place in the group, always
in true composition with the background of the scene.
For picturesqueness of manner, note so trivial a thing
as the turn of his hand in beckoning from a window, in
" Ruy Blas," to a personage down in an outer court-
yard to come up ; or his assumption of the *Duke's*
livery in the same scene ; or his writing a letter from
dictation.    In the last scene of Victor Hugo's noble
drama, his bearing becomes positively inspired ; and
his sudden assumption of the attitude of the heads-
man, in his denunciation of the *Duke* and threat to be
his executioner, is, so far as I know, one of the most
ferociously picturesque things conceivable on the stage.

The foregoing use of the word *ferociously* reminds
me to remark that this artist is a master of passionate vehemence ; in which aspect he appears to me
to represent, perhaps more than any other, an interesting union of characteristics of two great nations, the
French and the Anglo-Saxon.[1]    Born in London of a
French mother, by a German father, but reared entirely
in England and in France, there is, in his fury, a combination of French suddenness and impressibility with
our more slowly demonstrative Anglo-Saxon way when
we get, as we say, " our blood up," that produces an
intensely fiery result.    The fusion of two races is in
it, and one cannot decidedly say that it belongs to
either ; but one can most decidedly say that it belongs
to a powerful concentration of human passion and
emotion, and to human nature.

[1] This is a mistake ; Fechter's mother was Piemontese.

Mr. Fechter has been in the main more accustomed to speak French than to speak English, and therefore he speaks our language with a French accent. But whosoever would suppose that he does not speak English fluently, plainly, distinctly, and with a perfect understanding of the meaning, weight, and value of every word, would be greatly mistaken. Not only is his knowledge of English — extending to the most subtle idiom or the most recondite cant phrase — more extensive than that of many of us who have English for our mother tongue, but his delivery of Shakespeare's blank verse is remarkable, facile, musical, and intelligent. To be in a sort of pain for him, as one sometimes is for a foreigner speaking English, or to be in any doubt of his having twenty synonymes at his tongue's end if he should want one, is out of the question after having been of his audience.

A few words of two of his Shakespearian impersonations, and I shall have indicated enough in advance of Mr. Fechter's presentation of himself. That quality of picturesqueness, on which I have already laid stress, is strikingly developed in his *Iago ;* and yet it is so judiciously governed that his *Iago* is not in the least picturesque according to the conventional ways of frowning, sneering, diabolically grinning, and elaborately doing everything else that would induce *Othello* to run him through the body very early in the play. Mr. Fechter is the *Iago* who could and did make friends ; who could dissect his master's soul without flourishing his scalpel as if it were a walking-stick ; who could overpower *Emilia* by other arts than a sign of the Saracen's Head grimness; who could be a boon companion without *ipso facto* warning all beholders off by the portentous phenomenon; who could sing a song and clink a can naturally enough, and stab men really in the dark, — not in a transparent notification of himself as going about seeking whom to stab.   Mr. Fechter's *Iago* is no more in the conventional psychological mode than in the conventional hussar pantaloons and boots; and you shall see the picturesqueness of his wearing borne out in his bearing all through the tragedy, down to the moment when he becomes invincibly and consistently dumb.

Perhaps no innovation in art was ever accepted with so much favor by so many intellectual persons, precommitted to and preoccupied by another system, as Mr. Fechter's *Hamlet*.   I take this to have been the case (as it unquestionably was in London), not because of its picturesqueness, not because of its novelty, not because of its many scattered beauties, but because of its perfect consistency with itself.   As the animal painter said of his favorite picture of rabbits, that "there was more nature about those rabbits than you usually found in rabbits," so it may be said of Mr. Fechter's *Hamlet*, that there was more consistency about that *Hamlet* than you usually found in *Hamlets*.

Its great and satisfying originality was in its possessing the merit of a distinctly conceived and executed idea.   From the first appearance of the broken glass of fashion and mould of form, pale and worn with weeping for his father's death, and remotely suspicious of its cause, to his final struggle with *Horatio* for the fatal cup, there were cohesion and coherence in Mr. Fechter's view of the character.

Devrient, the German actor, had, some years before in London, fluttered the theatrical doves considerably by such changes as being seated when instructing the players, and like mild departures from established usage ; but he had worn, in the main, the old nondescript dress, and had held forth, in the main, in the old way, hovering between sanity and madness. I do not remember whether he wore his hair crisply curled short, as if he were going to an everlasting dancing-master's party at the Danish Court, but I do remember that most other *Hamlets* since the great Kemble have been bound to do so. Mr. Fechter's *Hamlet*, a pale woebegone Norseman with long flaxen hair, wearing a strange garb never associated with the part upon the English stage (if ever seen there at all), and making a piratical swoop upon the whole fleet of little theatrical prescriptions without meaning, — or, like Dr. Johnson's celebrated friend, with only one idea in them and that a wrong one, — never could have achieved its extraordinary success but for its animation by one pervading purpose to which all changes were made intelligibly subservient. The bearing of this purpose on the treatment of *Ophelia*, on the death of *Polonius*, and on the old student fellowship between *Hamlet* and *Horatio*, was exceedingly striking ; and the difference between picturesqueness of stage arrangement for mere stage effect, and for the elucidation of a meaning, was well displayed in there having been a gallery of musicians at the play, and in one of them passing, on his way out, with his instrument in his hand, when *Hamlet*, seeing it, took it from him to point his talk with *Rosencrantz* and *Guildenstern*.

This leads me to the observation with which I have all along desired to conclude : that Mr. Fechter's romance and picturesqueness are always united to a true artist's intelligence and a true artist's training in a true artist's spirit. He became one of the company at the Théâtre Français when he was a very young man, and he has cultivated his natural gifts in the best schools. I cannot wish my friend a better audience than he will have in the American people, and I cannot wish them a better actor than they will have in my friend.

CHARLES DICKENS.

[*Atlantic Monthly*, August, 1869.]

—◆—

THERE was something so decidedly novel in Mr. Fechter's performance of *Hamlet*, and it so long remained a subject of interest, not only with his admirers but with those who questioned the correctness of his theory, that the announcement of his intended appearance as *Othello*, made several months since, has proved a source of general curiosity among the large body of literary playgoers who properly regard the representations of Shakespeare's characters as the highest test of histrionic excellence. Whether the more impassioned *Othello*, prompt in physical action, would appear to greater or less advantage under his treatment than the more reflective *Hamlet*, infirm of purpose, all might be certain that nothing commonplace or conventional would be witnessed, but that an intellectual and conscientious artist would present them with an interpretation not founded on stage tradition, but derived solely from a study of Shakespeare's text. Nor was curiosity disappointed by the fact that a private performance of " Othello," too complete to be termed a rehearsal, took place on Thursday night, in the presence of a numerous though select audience. Indeed, those who did not belong to the exclusive party on Tuesday were eager yesterday morning to question their more privileged friends ; and the anxiety to know the result of the first public performance, which took place last night, was rather heightened than quenched by the partial revelations of the previous evening.

An edition of " Othello," by Mr. Fechter, circulated on Tuesday and now regularly published, sufficed to show that in the entire conduct of the play a completely new ground would be taken. There is not in this edition a single explanatory note, but the minute stage directions, which even describe the emotions to be portrayed, amount to a psychological comment on the tragedy. German dramatists, of the Kotzebue school, wrote and printed their own stage directions on a similar principle, and have sometimes been ridiculed on that account, as they were charged with endeavoring to conceal the poverty of their dialogue by the wealth of their rubric. No such ridicule can attach to Mr. Fechter, who interprets an author already established as classical, and who wishes to show by precept, as well as by example, his notions how " Othello " ought to be represented.

The theory of Mr. Fechter, practically manifested last night, is not to be sought merely in his own performance of the principal character. The *Iago* of Mr. Ryder and the *Desdemona* of Miss Leclercq must be regarded as embodying to a certain extent the conceptions of the ingenious innovator ; for they must have been forced to unlearn all they retained of stage traditions before they could move easily in the path prescribed for them in the rehearsals. All these details of action which are technically expressed by the word *business* have been changed, and the work is presented under an aspect entirely new. People sit where they were wont to stand, are scattered about where they used to be huddled together, and reformed into picturesque groups where they once were marshalled into unvarying straight lines. When *Othello* hears the first insinuations of *Iago* he is quietly writing his despatches at a table ; when *Iago* utters his satire against woman, he is leaning on a pillar with his merry listeners gathered around him ; when the death of *Roderigo* takes place, it is with all the preparation and circumstances of a grand melodramatic murder ; and so on through the entire piece, — having in his preface declared war against " tradition " as the worm-eaten and unwholesome prison where dramatic art languishes in fetters.

[*London Times*, Oct. 24, 1861.]

MR. FECHTER skilfully simulates the tenderness and devotion of a new-made husband. The rapid transition of feeling, as he suddenly passes from the happy dalliance of love to the stern business of the camp, is also well marked ; and his severe reproof to his officers for managing their private and domestic quarrels in a town of war, where the people's hearts are brimful of fear, is delivered with impressive dignity of tone, manner, and aspect. The third act is, as every one knows, the grandest and most sublime in the tragedy. The beauties of Mr. Fechter's acting in this all-important portion of the play are neither few nor trivial. His blank look of horror when his torturer first infuses the poison of suspicion by means of the perfidious suggestion, "She did deceive her father, marrying you ; " his attempt to shake off his misgivings as a fearful dream ; his struggle to speak calmly while his agony is revealed by the little movements of his hands, the twitching of the muscles of his face, and the slight but fearful trembling of his veins ; the brief return of love to his bursting heart when *Desdemona* approaches him ; and the bitter anguish with which he refers to the afflictions he could have borne had his wife but remained true to him, — are all thrillingly visible to those whose proximity to the stage enables them to observe closely the play of the actor's features, and the significance of his minutest gesture. The profound dejection of his voice and manner when, in reply to *Iago's* proffers of sympathy, he exclaims with a sigh like a spasm, " Not a jot, not a jot," is perfectly heart-breaking ; and the proud disdain which swells in his bosom when he utters the humiliating words, "Set on thy wife to observe" is finely conceived and forcibly expressed. But his mode of exclaiming "O fool! fool! fool!" when he discovers how he has been abused, like one awakening from a trance of horrors of which he is scarcely conscious, and his last sad retrospect of the sorrows of his life and of the angelic qualities of his lost love, are most impressive; as also is the wild despair with which he hangs over the body of *Desdemona* and vainly calls upon her by name.

[*London Morning Post*, Oct. 21, 1861.]

———◆———

THE success which attended Mr. Fechter's assumption of the character of *Hamlet* last season completely accounts for the curiosity of the public, demonstrated in an unusually crowded house which was exhibited last night when he attempted *Othello*. The fact that Mr. Fechter played *Hamlet* seventy-five times proves the effect of his performance upon the general public. That he made a deep impression upon the most intellectual of playgoers, — and moreover upon a class of persons who of late have been accustomed to look upon theatrical exhibitions with a feeling nearly akin to contempt, — is also well known to most of those who have the opportunity of forming correct opinions on such matters.

In the first two acts *Othello* has little to do ; but in these, in the dignity with which he receives the reproaches of *Brabantio*, and in the frank, easy, yet persuasive delivery of the apology, the true dramatic artist could be seen. In the scene in which *Othello* interrupts and reproves the drunkenness of *Cassio*, the assumption of dignity to which we have been accustomed, and which was wanting in Mr. Fechter, was undoubtedly more effective, but less true to a natural view of the character. It is by the third act that every *Othello* must be tested. Here a striking change has been introduced ; it is not till late in the scene that *Othello* is made to yield to a suspicion of his wife's falsehood. He appears first to disregard or to utterly misunderstand the innuendoes of *Iago*, then to accept them as general reflections not applicable to himself any more than to any one else. Next, as they are reiterated, he becomes, in the simple honesty of his nature, completely puzzled ; but not till *Iago* alludes to *Brabantio's* early warning, in the lines " She did deceive her father, marrying you," does the actual suspicion strike him, as with a thunderstruck expression he exclaims, " And so she did." Mr. Fechter's utterance of " Not a jot, not a jot," was remarkably expressive, and drew forth one of the loudest bursts of applause of the evening. It is just after this that he catches a sight of his black face in the glass ; and, as *Iago* proceeds, he continually glances in the direction of the mirror, till he is worked up to request *Iago* to set on *Emilia* " to observe,"— immediately after suggesting which, an expression of the deepest shame breaks over his countenance. This new treatment of the scene affords room not for so much energy as we have witnessed, but for numerous delicate and subtle touches. Again, in the subsequent scene, the Farewell is accompanied with action most varied and expressive. The eager look with which *Othello* drinks in *Iago's* story of *Cassio's* dream was a remarkable instance of facial expression, and the agitation and excitement that goes on increasing throughout this scene was finely marked. Another fine passage was the Handkerchief scene with *Desdemona*. The intense expectation with which he watched the result of his first enquiry, the doubts, the delight with which for a moment he drew her to his bosom, where she says "it is not lost," with his subsequent repulse of her, and the towering passion of his demand for its production, were most effective; and the picture formed by the sudden appearance of *Emilia*, just as his arm is raised to strike *Desdemona*, made a most fitting close to this part of the scene. The fourth act, — where he receives the letter from the Senate, and behaves with such violence to his wife, — whilst equally effective, was rendered less than ordinarily painful by the evident strong feeling by which every tone and movement appears to be dictated.

[*London Morning Herald*, Oct. 24, 1861.]

————◆————

IT is not until the third act that Mr. Fechter puts forth any of his powers, and up to that period many celebrated speeches, hitherto known as points, fall

flatly enough upon the ear. The Address to the Senate
for instance, which has for so long held an Enfield's
Speakerish celebrity on oration days at minor schools,
is divested of all that rotundity of eloquence and pom-
pous manner hitherto allotted to it. In Mr. Fechter's
mouth it is simply an honest apology for a natural action
colloquially delivered. In the second act, too, there
is nothing specially noticeable saving the overweening
tenderness invariably displayed to *Desdemona*, and the
purely natural savage tone in which the "noisy bell"
is ordered to be silenced, during the drunken quarrel between *Cassio* and *Montano*. But the whole of the third
act, as far as *Othello* is concerned, sparkles into original
genius when *Iago* first asks about *Cassio's* acquaintance with *Desdemona*. *Othello* answers him lightly.
He is looking over some papers, and speaks at first almost at random. Then, finding his interlocutor repeating
his phrases and harping with full power on certain words,
he rallies him lightly and playfully. Not even when the
suggestion of his wife's infidelity is made, does he wince,
until *Iago* reminds him of the manner in which she
deceives her father. Then his face falls, and the avowal
"And so she did," comes in dreary heart-broken accents
from between his parted lips. The entire scene is re-
plete with beauties. Nothing can be finer than the
touch of nature conveyed in the tone in which he replies "Not a jot, not a jot," when *Iago* hints that he
has dashed his spirits ; nothing more suggestive than the
abrupt stop which the noble-hearted *Moor* comes to when
the hint, so loathsome to his real nature, — that *Emilia*
should be set on to watch *Desdemona*, — first rises to his

lips ; nothing grander than the gradual rousing of his rage during *Iago's* recital of *Cassio's* dream, and the vehement burst with which he declares that he *will* be satisfied of his wife's fidelity.

It is in touches of this kind — and there are dozens of them throughout the play — that **Mr.** Fechter's genius is shown.

[*London Daily News*, Oct. 24, 1861.]

———◆———

IN the third act, and especially in the scene where his jealousy is first aroused by *Iago*, the powers of the actor began to be displayed. Nothing could be finer than the constrained calmness with which he attempts to defend himself from the accusation of being depressed by the suspicions the tempter has aroused in his mind. The apparently commonplace words " Not a jot, not a jot " were never uttered in a tone of truer pathos. Then again when, more and more persuaded of his wife's infidelity, he begs *Iago* to place *Emilia* as a spy upon *Desdemona*, the expression of shame and anguish that immediately followed was most finely rendered. Both these points were at once observed by the audience, and the applause elicited was of the most enthusiastic character.

In the second scene of the fourth act, too, *Othello's* burst of tender pathos, after denouncing *Desdemona* as false, had all the effect of a sudden inspiration, and touched the sympathies of the entire house. In the last act Mr. Fechter gave singular significance to the opening lines of the scene, " It is the cause, it is the cause, my soul," by glancing at himself in the mirror as he spoke, as though exposing *Desdemona's* frailty by the color of his face, — thus recurring to an idea expressed in a previous part of the play.

Throughout the representation it was easy to see that an original mind had been at work, and this not only in one character but in all ; and we believe we are justified in stating that to Mr. Fechter are due the many novelties introduced into the stage arrangements of the piece. Nearly all, in fact, of what is called by actors the business of the tragedy, is entirely new.

[*London Daily Telegraph*, Oct. 24, 1861.]

# INDEX.